P9-EL

DO NOT REMOVE
CARDS FROM POCKET

10-3-94

Eight Women of the YWCA

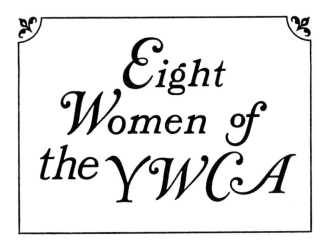

by

Marion O. Robinson

Preface by Mary French Rockefeller

National Board of the Young Women's Christian Association of the U.S.A.

New York, 1966

$\mathcal{P}$reface

AT THIS TIME in our history when we are searching for new ways to restate values, it is important for us to know our heritage and see what those values were that our founders fought for and helped to create in the YWCA. May their vision throw more light on present concerns and help us look toward the future with confidence and a sense of adventure.

Many people have participated in forwarding the work of the YWCA. In this book we have selected eight women, both Board and Staff, to make more vivid for those who never knew them the times and efforts of hundreds. In telling something about them as persons, their motivations, the obstacles they met and how they surmounted them, and something of their work in the organization, all against the background of their times, we hope it will help YWCA leaders of today and tomorrow to feel continuity with these early leaders and to find courage to meet the problems and changes of their own times.

Of the women we have chosen to tell about, four were charter members of the National Board, three were members of the original National Board staff, and the eighth came to the Board after World War I and gave outstanding service for more than thirty-five years, primarily in the international work. One of the eight served on the staff for five years, became a Board member, was President of both the YWCA and the National Board and is still active as an honorary Board member. Since we have tried to convey a feeling for the personalities of the women, we have used as illustrations, wherever possible, photographs showing them in informal moments.

Those of us who worked on the planning of this book felt there was now a real opportunity to gather the facts about these women by means of interviews and correspondence with their families and close friends, and we greatly appreciate their valuable help. We were most fortunate to obtain the services of Miss Marion O. Robinson, who has written about the eight in such a delightful way. Miss Robinson, a long-time member of the YWCA, a member of The Authors League of America and a specialist in writing about social welfare, health and medical topics, has carried out a number of important YWCA writing and editing assignments over the last fifteen years.

I want particularly to thank Mrs. Harrison S. Elliott and Miss Mary S. Sims for reading the manuscript and giving us the benefit of their experience and knowledge of YWCA history. Mrs. Elliott has said, "Often when I have gone into the Assembly Room at 600 Lexington Avenue alone, I have felt the presence of women who are no longer physically with us, women who have left to us the responsibility for the next stages of what they dreamed and brought into being." They have indeed left us a bright torch to carry and to hand on to the next generation.

The faith, vision and concern for meeting the needs of women and girls, not only in this country but around the world, are evidenced by all those who join the YWCA to learn from one another, help one another and try in a meaningful way to discover an identity and purpose in their lives. As new needs arise that involve the role of women in their homes and local communities and in the world—whether these needs be for improved education, basic literacy, the advancement of health and nutrition, or vocational training—the YWCA is contributing today with enthusiasm and interest through its many programs built on a foundation of values that endure.

Mary French Rockefeller

September, 1966

Contents

Illustrations

The author wishes to thank members of the families and friends of the "Eight Women of the YWCA" and the National Board for kindly making available the photographs used in this volume.

This volume is dedicated to the women of the YWCA all over the world.

Women of the Era: YWCA war workers on their way overseas in 1917 march past National Board headquarters in New York. Florence Simms stands at far right, on third step. (BELOW) Emma Bailey Speer, Theresa Wilbur Paist and Mary Billings French at a 1924 Washington meeting of the World's Committee of the YWCA.

CHAPTER ONE

'Should Women Learn the Alphabet?'

THE COLLECTIVE ENTHUSIASM, intelligence, independent spirit and religious motivation of hundreds of women from all parts of the country went into the making of the YWCA of the U.S.A. This series of profiles, vignettes, sketches—call them what you will—describes a very small group of women who took leadership in shaping the YWCA in its first two decades as a united, national movement. What they accomplished would not have been remotely possible if it had not been for the scores of other women who thought, talked and prayed with them; who supported, challenged and opposed them; who traveled and worked with them; and the many across the country who may never have known them personally but nonetheless had a bond with them—the bond of shared concerns. The names of only a few of the many who played other important roles in those historic years will appear in these pages. To see the whole picture of the YWCA's "goodly heritage," the reader must keep visualizing in the background of these brief sketches the hosts of women who helped make the YWCA what it was and is.

These eight women were born and brought up in the latter half of the 19th Century—three in Eastern United States, four in the Midwest, one on the West Coast. Most of them were only a generation or two removed from pioneer ancestry, and all of them came from homes where religion and education were highly valued. Five were college or university graduates, and a sixth attended a woman's college for three years.

Theirs was the generation that saw America change from a country of farms and villages to a country of cities. In their growing-up years, the industrial revolution was also coming of age. It was a period much like our own in some ways—inventive, comparatively fast-paced, and shot through with controversy. Materialism vied with humanitarianism, and privilege with disadvantage.

The men and women of the West were still pushing back America's rough frontiers. The Eastern cities, teeming with immigrants and empire builders, struggled to provide for mushrooming populations the necessities of urban living—pure water, sewage disposal, police protection, adequate lighting, transportation. City life was replacing the post-office box with free mail-carrier service; and the first modern apartment houses were being built.

Early versions of the means of communication which now link all parts of the United States with each other and with every country in the world appeared. In Boston, Alexander Graham Bell dreamed up the telephone; in Milwaukee, C. E. Sholes worked at perfecting the typewriter (for which Mark Twain, an early customer, paid $125 and reported, "It piles up an awful stack of words on one page, and of course, saves paper."). Cyrus W. Fields succeeded in laying the first trans-Atlantic cable, although this could not have been readily available to the general population, since it cost the Associated Press $5,800 to receive a speech by King William of Prussia to his Parliament! The numbers of daily newspapers more than doubled between 1880 and 1900. Weeklies and semiweeklies serving the rural towns increased from nine thousand to fourteen thousand. The rapid spread of schools, bookstores and libraries, as well as magazines and newspapers, made America, in the phrase of one historian, "the land of the general reader."

Nowhere were the revolutionary changes of this era felt more keenly than in the life of women. Into their homes came the first time- and labor-saving devices: the egg beater, the double boiler, aluminum cookware, the washing machine, the sewing machine. Into their cupboards went the first packaged cereals, canned fruit, vegetables, meats. For many years it was thought that only a lazy housewife would feed her family baker's bread, and that it was poor taste to wear factory-made housedresses instead of stitching them up at home; but most women rejoiced, even if they had to do it secretly, at the benefits that accrued to them from these early days of the machine age.

"Soon even cookbooks may become obsolete," chortled a writer in a woman's magazine in 1887, "as each can has a label with directions how to cook."

Now, too, for the first time, substantial numbers of women began to choose work outside the home either for reasons of economic freedom or self-fulfillment, instead of occupying their traditional niche in society.

By the close of the Civil War, hundreds were entering professions or were employed in industry. The influence of Florence Nightingale had leaped the ocean and, supported by the example of Clara Barton, soon led to the opening of schools of nursing in four Eastern hospitals. The first women's medical college (in Philadelphia) had been turning out graduates for fourteen years. Women were building careers as actresses, singers, sculptresses and journalists. One of the latter, indignant at being excluded because of her sex from a press dinner for Charles Dickens, promptly went out and organized one of the first women's clubs.

It was a time of unprecedented prosperity—except during the black days of the Panic of '73 and the recovery period which followed—for great numbers of people; the exceptions were some of the rural residents and grossly underpaid labor. Commerce and industry were in the hands of men—many of them devoted church members of all denominations—to whom pairs of hands were part of the equipment of production, just as were parts of machinery and tons of steel; and the law of supply and demand ruled supreme. Activities of the early labor unions were regarded as unwarranted interference by these industrialists, most of whom had built their businesses with their own hard labor and sheer nerve, and they felt deeply that this fact alone justified their point of view.

When peace came after the Civil War, ordinary workmen were glad to get $2 a day for a ten-hour day. Women workers in shops, factories and large stores earned $3.50 or $4 weekly, but still counted themselves fortunate when compared with those who carried materials home and made shirts and overalls for seventy-five cents a dozen. An American historian reports, "Girls in the drygoods stores of the great Eastern cities where civilization was the proudest of its achievements, toiled from seven-thirty in the morning until the closing hour of nine or ten, without seats, without restrooms or facilities for a quiet lunch . . . and for this health-ruining drudgery many were paid five dollars a week." But the lure of the city and even very small cash wages touched alike the hustler who wanted to—and in those days, could—build an empire from a few dollars, the farm girl who fashioned dreams of her own from her brother's Horatio Alger books, and the immigrant who looked for a new life in the land of opportunity.

Women were the storm center of several controversies, one being their right to higher education. Men distrusted the idea. According to an American historian, "When an ambitious girl of 1865 looked about her, she found only three or four institutions, Oberlin the most notable, of worthy standards." Tempers and temperatures rose when the matter was discussed, even among faculty members of the great universities who predicted nervous breakdowns for the women who tackled advanced curricula. Thomas W. Higginson, a Unitarian minister, early abolitionist and friend of the feminist movement, was so put out with the arguments advanced against women's education that he wrote a sarcastic essay for the *Atlantic Monthly* titled "Should Women Learn the Alphabet?" In the midst of these viewings with alarm, in the decade between 1865 and 1876, the money to establish Vassar, Smith and Wellesley was given, respectively, by a brewer, a spinster and a lawyer.

In 1848 Elizabeth Cady Stanton and her friends at Seneca Falls, New York, had fired the opening gun of the woman suffrage movement, but most people refused to take it seriously until after the Civil War. Then, in view of their war services, many women believed they had as much right to the ballot as the liberated Negroes, and some men began to pay attention to the idea, too.

"We speak in schoolhouses, barns, sawmills, and log cabins, with boards for seats and lanterns hung around for lights," wrote Susan B. Anthony during a campaign in Kansas, "but people come twenty miles to hear us." On election day ten thousand men of that Western state cast their vote for equal suffrage for women—not a majority vote, but a substantial minority one.

In spite of the prevailing arguments that, given the vote, women would no longer be regarded with reverence, that family life would be unsettled by sex equality, that feminine intellect was incapable of dealing with civic issues, several Western territories gave women complete political equality, and some states granted them the right to vote in school elections.

By 1890 when two parallel national organizations realized they were "two blades of the same scissors" and united as the National American Woman Suffrage Association, considerable progress had been made. Although it would be another thirty years before the Nineteenth Amendment became an accomplished fact, the controversy generated by the movement was bestowing upon women a new sense of themselves. The men who were in opposition because it "put ideas into women's heads" were perfectly right. It did.

Besides enjoying the fruits of the factory which lightened their household burdens, entering the working world and stepping toward educational and political equality, women were busily joining groups of all kinds. Many went into the temperance movement which, by 1880, was one of the real powers of the land; many joined clubs.

"We have art clubs, book clubs, dramatic clubs, pottery clubs. We have sewing circles, philanthropic associations, scientific, religious, athletic, musical and decorative art societies," reported a woman contributor to *Atlantic Monthly in* 1880.

All of these symptoms of women's struggle toward an easier, more self-respecting and self-reliant footing in American society were, of course, the subject of considerable comment. While one man wrote in *Century* that "the crowning glory of the present age is that every woman is free to develop her own personality," others wrote about "The Transitional American Woman," or "The Restlessness of the Age," in which the author said the great fault of the girl of the day [1890] was discontent. "She calls it by a more magnificent sounding name of ambition, but in reality she is absolutely restless and dissatisfied with whatever may be her position in life."

One of the groups women were joining was the Young Women's Christian Association. Although, as in the women's suffrage movement, it was four decades from the time the first YWCA to use the name as such was organized in Boston until it became a genuine united, national movement, its appeal to Christian women of humanitarian bent won hundreds of members from 1866 onward.

The first YWCAs sprang up in rapid succession in the large cities of the East, Middle Atlantic and Midwest states. To the second meeting of YWCA representatives, in Philadelphia in

1873, thirty-six Associations sent either delegates or reports of program since the 1871 meeting. Soon afterward the conference adopted a constitution as the International Board of the YWCA. The year of the Philadelphia meeting, a student YWCA was organized at Normal University, in Illinois, and other campuses in the Midwest quickly followed suit. YMCA leaders encouraged and assisted the women students in forming these Associations, which were patterned after the men's organization.

In 1881 representatives of the student Associations received the blessing of the International Board to promote YWCA work in colleges and seminaries. Twice in the next ten years the student group, which in the meantime established a national organization named the American Committee of the YWCA, with headquarters in Chicago, proposed, in effect, a merger, and both times the International Board rejected the proposals.

Several factors stood in the way. There was a lack of understanding between the students on the one hand and the more mature women on the other, and because the two movements were predominantly rooted in different sections—the American Committee in the Midwest and the International Board in the East. But these proved to be superficial differences. A difference that came closer to the bone, but at the time was discussed only in private conversations, was the American Committee's close ties with the YMCA. The International Board took great pride in itself as an independently developing woman's movement. Events later proved that their widely differing programs could become part of the same organization, but at that moment each was imbued with its own strong sense of purpose—the students to win young women through evangelistic meetings and Bible study to "a life of Christian service at home or in the mission field," and the women of the International Board to provide services under Christian auspices to meet the physical, educational, recreational and spiritual needs of young women who were "dependent on their own exertions for support."

The difference that became a critical issue concerned the basis for YWCA membership. Like their YMCA brethren, the women students of the American Committee required their members to be members of a Protestant evangelical church, and in their proposals to the International Board made it clear that they would expect a merged organization to adopt this basis. The International Board left the membership basis to the discretion of its local Associations. Thus, some required such church membership of all members, some only of office-holders, and some made no stipulation at all. In a number of the latter group, Unitarians and Roman Catholics were welcome as members and often held office, and many members had no church affiliation. The board placed great value on "the fellowship of many who have long been most earnest and sympathetic co-workers," and told American Committee representatives they would not want to lose it.

Finally, there was a difference of organizational philosophy. The International Board strongly believed in complete autonomy of its local Associations, employed almost no professional staff, and its headquarters was wherever the current president lived. It was so loosely organized that one of its members once referred to it as "a rope of sand." The American Committee maintained a headquarters office with a constantly increasing professional staff, some of whom were organized to follow local work closely on a state-by-state basis, and had begun what is called today an in-service training program for professional workers. As it expanded the American Committee began to work in cities and towns as well as on campuses.

While the two organizations paralleled each other's work in some respects, each was laying the groundwork for important aspects of the organization that was to be. Eastern city Associations of the International Board started residences for young women, as well as the many-faceted city YWCA programs, and began a service for women arriving by ship in East Coast ports that later became the Travelers' Aid Society. At the same time, the American Committee, as a natural step growing out of its association with the World Student Christian Federation, participated in forming the World's YWCA in 1894 and recruited its first General Secretary, Annie M. Reynolds, a New England-born American.

A jurisdictional dispute was bound to occur, and it finally came in 1904 in Washington, D.C., where the International Board operated a women's boarding home used chiefly by older women. A group of younger women appealed to the American Committee to organize a program more suitable for them, and a representative, Emma Hayes, was dispatched to visit them. Following the visit, during which plans for an American Committee-sponsored program were begun, the young women invited members of the International Board to meet with them for a Day of Prayer service, thinking it a good occasion for promoting Christian fellowship. The two groups met at a hotel, and a member of the hostess group, a woman lawyer, presided. In the midst of the meeting a messenger appeared at the door, walked up to the chairman and presented her with a legal document which she saw at once was an injunction. Hastily, she dismissed the meeting. The injunction proved to have been secured by the International Board to prevent the American Committee from continuing its organization in Washington.

It was a real crisis. No one was more keenly aware of that fact than a New York City woman who was not even a member of the YWCA. Grace Dodge, a forty-nine-year-old spinster, philanthropist, champion of education, friend of working women, had watched the development of the YWCA closely, had addressed its meetings and conferences, but had declined to join the board of either organization. Her reason: she had foreseen the crisis long before and knew that when it came, she could be of more assistance as an outsider than as a member. Now she arranged to see one of the secretaries whom she knew well, telling her she saw the situation not as a "one-city affair," but as a "matter of national concern," and offering, if both groups wished it, to serve as mediator.

The YWCA as it exists today came out of meetings and mediation that followed, introducing the era of Grace Dodge, Mabel Cratty, Emma Bailey Speer, Mary Billings French, Vera Scott Cushman, Martha Boyden Finley, Florence Simms and Theresa Wilbur Paist.

CHAPTER TWO

$\mathcal{G}$race H. Dodge

Mediator and Mentor

IF SHE HAD BEEN BORN in the Twentieth Century, she might have been a college president, a member of Congress or perhaps a great financier. Her brother said if she had been born a man, she would have been a general. When she died, J. Pierpont Morgan said of her, "She had the finest business brain in the United States, not excepting that of any man."

As it happened, she was born May 21, 1856, the oldest of a family of six children who constituted the fourth generation of an old and wealthy New York family. Among her forebears on both sides of the family were men who dealt in vast business and financial enterprises, always combined with leadership in civic affairs and religious institutions. Her great grandfather, David Low Dodge, founded the New York Peace Society, said to be the first American organization of its kind.

The Dodge family life was close and loving. William E. Dodge, Jr., who called his daughter "Gracie," liked to gather his children together in the evenings and tell them stories, after which they would learn new hymns to sing together. Although he was a true Victorian father, he took great pride in his daughter's keen mind; even as a child, she was allowed to sit quietly in the room and listen when he met with associates to discuss business, civic and church matters, and as time went on he invited her opinions and discussed these matters with her as an equal. This early training, combined with the teaching of her governess, Miss Flint, who drilled her in spelling and put great stress on her learning punctuality and attention to detail, and required her to write at least one letter each day, developed in her those mental and personal habits which became outstanding characteristics in later years.

For her mother, the young Grace felt a wistful admiration, for she was comely, graceful and charming, while Grace herself was, even as a child, unusually large and heavy. Her brother "Cleve" teased her about her size, beginning his letters from prep school "Dear Little Giant," and although she dearly loved her brothers and sisters and, beginning at age fifteen, took increasing responsibility for their care because of her mother's illness, it was many years before she stopped being sensitive and began laughing about it herself.

Home for the Dodge children was a large house at 39th Street and Madison Avenue from which they ventured out on fine days with their Irish nurse, Bella, to watch the dashing traffic of horse-drawn carriages and to enjoy the street singers, the calls of hucksters and the stir of a city bustling with the activities of a major seaport and business and financial center. They saw the first steam fire engines careening on their way, the great golden chariot which heralded Van Amburgh's circus and, one sad day when Grace was nine years old, the somber procession carrying the body of the martyred President Lincoln on its way to the Illinois-bound train.

When the children were still quite young, Mr. Dodge built Greystone, a great Victorian summer home in Riverdale, then a small community quite far north of the city boundary. Situated in a forty-acre woodland area, the house overlooked the Hudson River and the New Jersey Palisades. The comfortable house and the open countryside where she could ride her pony, Nettie, became another home very quickly to young Grace. Later it was to become a haven of peace and gracious hospitality as well as a workshop for the many people with whom she was associated in a series of large dreams which became grand realities.

When she stepped into the stream of YWCA life in 1905, Grace Dodge had for thirty years been involved in educational and social welfare enterprises which, in sweep and scope, matched the mercantile enterprises of her father and grandfathers. Six feet tall, she was a big-boned woman with heavy jaw, expressive, intelligent hazel eyes, and light chestnut brown hair which she wore piled on top of her head. She retained the simplicity, directness and modesty of her girlhood days, but the years had changed her shyness to reserve, her awkwardness to poise and a commanding presence, her self-conscious sensitiveness to warmth of interest in people.

To her lifelong regret, her father had vetoed college for her in favor of a finishing school, then considered more appropriate for a wellborn young lady. At Miss Porter's School in Farmington, Connecticut, which she attended for a year and a half in her sixteenth and seventeenth years, she enjoyed meeting girls from other parts of the country, but felt restless and out of place. She left school to accompany her parents on a six-month European trip and never returned to formal education. Increasing responsibility for running the house had fallen to her because of her mother's poor health, and she was happier as homemaker and hostess, although continuously searching for her niche in life. She told her father that she would like to go into business, but he replied that "women don't go into such fields," and he bade her remember the family tradition of *noblesse oblige* and that wealth such as theirs constituted a trust to help others. She took him at his word. When plans for her coming out party were broached, she asked instead that her parents give a series of luncheons and dinner parties with "people who have done things to help others so I can learn from them." They agreed.

Thus began a unique career which in forty years would touch

the lives of thousands and benefit a great number of national and international institutions. The eighteen-year-old Grace Dodge began a Work Book in which facts about the various projects in which she was involved were entered in an orderly, concise fashion. Her talents proved to be those of the builder, the developer, the organizer, and everything she touched seemed to flourish and grow. A modest library she started in the Greystone greenhouse for the gardener and other neighborhood workmen grew into a community library in Riverdale. The Working Girls Society she helped girls of her Sunday School class to organize grew in less than ten years to seventy-five clubs with more than 2,100 members. A social worker wrote once that in fostering these self-governing clubs with their education, health and recreation programs, she had "thrown the first cable across the chasm that separated the daughters of the rich and the poor."

The work of which she was proudest began in 1876 with a small program to teach homemaking skills to disadvantaged girls and developed by 1884 into the Industrial Education Association, a sort of 19th Century Job Corps effort, which influenced the city's public schools to add industrial training to the curriculum. This work prompted the New York City mayor in 1886 to appoint Miss Dodge one of the first two women commissioners of education. Within a year she had made and presented a thoroughgoing study of technical training that established the urgent need for teacher education. She was in the vanguard of the move to establish the New York College for Training of Teachers, chartered in 1889, and was its moral and financial mainstay as well as its treasurer until long after it became Teachers College. "I dreamed that college once," she remarked proudly years later to a friend as they drove past the imposing building on the Columbia University campus.

By the turn of the century, her main concerns were two: to foster improvement of education, which to her was the source of the greatest satisfaction in living; and to safeguard the health and well being of the American girl. She helped plan an investigation of white slave traffic, the report of which opened the way for protective legislation, and lent her organizational skill to the mergers of small agencies which brought into being the American Social Hygiene Association and the Travelers Aid Society. Soon after 1900 she "went international," becoming a partner in the effort to put the American College for Women in Turkey on a sound footing and underwriting the expenses of the first woman secretary of the World Student Christian Federation, Miss Ruth Rouse.

As a philanthropist, she was no mere check-signer. She knew well each person and each program detail of each endeavor she supported, often combining business discussions with social occasions. The men and women of her devoted household staff were in her confidence and felt themselves part of each enterprise. Her home was open to nieces, nephews and neighborhood children with whom she had a deep bond of affection and understanding. With it all, those who were closest to her knew Grace Dodge as a lonely person who kept her strong emotions under stern control.

From May 24, 1905, when she first met with the officers of the two YWCA organizations until her death in 1914, the unity and growth of the YWCA of the U.S.A. was her major concern. The feelings of the women who accepted her invitation to meet and lunch with her at Hotel Manhattan in New York City that May day can be imagined. The issue that had divided them—whether to require membership in a Protestant evangelical church of YWCA members—was still unsettled and paramount. Members of the American Committee still smarted under the rebuffs they had had from the International Board, whose members in turn distrusted the employed secretaries of their "sister" organization, fearing the "evil" effect of professionalization. They also foresaw and resented the possibility of "national supervision."

Miss Dodge, who knew and admired her guests, sympathized deeply with both groups. Mabel Cratty, who was to become her "staff partner" in the days ahead, wrote of her, "She had a sheltering mind. . . . To every person conscious of sharp differences of opinion or of alien points of view, there was refuge in her presence . . . shelter for the opinions of all."

It is worthwhile today to review how she went about her task as mediator between the American Committee and the International Board. She opened the meeting by reading the prayer of Jesus in which He prayed that His followers might be made perfect in unity; then, after announcing that because of home duties she would leave at a stated time, she asked each woman in turn if she thought it better to have one organization. Each answered yes. "Then if you, the officers, wish it, it can be done," she summed up. A working agreement on the thorny issue of the basis for membership was reached and the meeting adjourned for luncheon.

A hostess *par excellence,* Miss Dodge had spared no effort. Flowers, good food and fine service did their work, and she helped them along. "She had a great gift," says a member of the original National Board staff, "of talking about trifles at just the right time to relieve tension. You wouldn't have thought such an analytically-minded person could be good at small talk, too, but she was. It was because she was so interested in people." In an atmosphere of relaxed comfort, the officers began to find each other quite pleasant and to see the advantage of working together.

After luncheon a second sore point was disposed of. Following a report on the Washington dispute between the American Committee and the International Board, Miss Dodge, with the consent of the group, appointed a woman from each of the two organizations to meet with an existing Washington committee, and it was agreed to allow both groups to continue their programs, forming a central committee to conduct a finance campaign. It was recommended that the Washington committee formulate "a plan of cooperation that will allow the YWCA to stand before the public as one movement."

By four o'clock plans were complete for appointment of a Joint Committee, with Miss Dodge as chairman, to work out the details of the many issues and questions involved in uniting the two organizations, and dates were set for the committee's first progress reports to both organizations.

In her usual courteous way, Miss Dodge thanked the women for being her guests and went off to her "home duties," which on this day began with taking her mother for a drive.

During the next ten months, a long list of individuals and groups from both organizations met with Miss Dodge at Greystone to consult about ways and means for the Joint Committee to do its job. From Chicago, Theresa Wilbur, a secretary in the student department of the American Committee, journeyed to New York with other staff members.

"Eleven of us met Miss Dodge together," she recalls. "We were all agog. If the plan for uniting the two organizations went through, we would be the nucleus of the national staff. I was in awe of Miss Dodge before I saw her. I expected because she was very rich, she would be self-centered and probably extremely stylish. The first surprise was her appearance; she was so big, so plain and so plainly dressed. The second surprise was how fast she won us over, telling us about her work on the New York City School Board. We could see it was true when she said, 'I have suffered in the cause of young women.' "

No voice went unheard in this period of consultation. Miss Dodge asked that she have the opportunity to talk with those who were "most bitter," as well as those who were most enthusiastic, and made it clear that, when necessary, she would underwrite travel costs.

In March, 1906, she called the Joint Committee together. From then until the convention was called the women worked intensively, preparing material and exhibits to go to the Associations. By convention time there was, says Mary S. Sims, the National Board historian, "general understanding of the nature, the privileges and the obligations which would be assumed by the new body," and applications for charter membership in the new organization had been made by 147 city and 469 student Associations.

The convention met in New York City's Old South Church on December 5, and was called together by Miss Dodge as chairman of the Joint Committee. Following the report of the nominating committee, she was elected president of the convention. The detailed report of the Joint Committee was presented and discussed by the 392 delegates representing 132 city and college Associations. By the end of the second day, December 6, the report had been accepted and the first National Board of thirty members had been elected. On December 7, the board met and elected Grace Dodge its president.

The Young Women's Christian Associations of the United States of America, chosen by the convention as the official name, had as its object "to unite in one body . . . to establish, develop and unify (the existing Associations); to advance the physical, social, intellectual, moral and spiritual interests of young women; to participate in the work of the World's Young Women's Christian Association."

The president of the new National Board began her work December 8. Mabel Cratty was appointed general secretary, and there began the partnership of two leaders who "welded the whole thing together for a wonderful movement," to quote a charter board member.

In the months that followed Miss Dodge's dreams for the YWCA began to take shape. Just as she had seen Teachers College become a research center for the science of teaching, she saw the headquarters of the YWCA as a "great research center for the study of the basic facts that concern the lives of girls and women"—a center that would make these facts available to all girls and women for the enrichment of their lives. One of the board's first ventures was to commission a sociologist at Adelphi College to make a study of wage-earning women. From the earliest days of the Joint Committee, Miss Dodge had taken it for granted the YWCA would have salaried executives for whom there should be a training system. She referred to the secretary-ships enthusiastically as "a new profession among women," and encouraged her fellow board members to share her great respect for the college-trained women of the staff.

With the help of theologians, instructors in social work and the *avant garde* of social reformers of the day, a curriculum on the graduate level was worked out, using the experience of the American Committee's successful Bible study courses in Chicago. Elizabeth Wilson, executive of the National Board's Secretarial Department, wrote that Miss Dodge "showed interest in every detail of blocking out the courses, forming the faculty and staff, arranging business matters, renting and equipping the house at Number 3 Gramercy Park." The National YWCA Training School opened in September, 1908, and by 1923, a few years before it closed, it had a fourteen-member faculty and eleven lecturers, and well over four hundred young women had passed through its portals, including students from twenty foreign countries.

"It was an old brownstone house," reminisces a member of the class of 1911, "with high ceilings and a stained glass window in the dining room. There were about twenty of us, all ages, some college graduates, some experienced YWCA workers. The principal, Miss Caroline Dow, was a Vassar graduate and a fine musician. She had the ways of a lady, and gave somewhat the atmosphere of a finishing school by conveying to us certain elegancies which might be missing from our previous education. I remember her telling us that when visiting in a board member's home, we must never put our combs and brushes on the bedroom dresser without slipping a piece of tissue paper underneath! She was a handsome woman and when she swept down the stairs at dinnertime, dressed to the nines, she was indeed an admirable figure. The students wore suits or long skirts with overblouses. After dinner we gathered around the fireplace, frequently to talk with guests—clergymen, social workers, people interested in social reforms.

"It was said the neighborhood folks referred to us as 'the house of nuns.' It is my recollection that we were most un-nunlike in our curiosity when David Graham Phillips, the muckraking journalist and novelist, was murdered in broad daylight in the spring of 1911 as he came out of the Princeton Club only a stone's throw from our house on Gramercy Park.

"The backbone of the curriculum was the study of Biblical literature, and history and philosophy of religion. The resident Bible instructor, later the dean, was Charlotte Adams. She was a graduate of Cornell and had done independent study of the Bible before attending the United Free Church College in Glasgow, Scotland, the first woman ever to be admitted there. Modern in her teaching, she was the first person I ever heard interpret the Biblical miracles as having symbolic meaning, which gave us a feeling for the scope of religion as nothing else had. She could be irascible, but painlessly so, and had great respect for mental ability in her students."

The Training School figured large in the plans for the headquarters building, another of Miss Dodge's long-range projects. In fact, for some time it was known as the National Training School Building, and the entrance facade at 135 East 52nd Street, originally the school entrance, is similar in size and decoration to the so-called main entrance at 600 Lexington Avenue.

Many people, including some husbands, did some headshaking when the land at the corner of Lexington Avenue and 52nd Street was chosen. It was surrounded by tenement houses, and a block away, the New York Central Railroad tracks ran aboveground straight up Park Avenue. Nevertheless, a board member, Mrs. Finley Shepard, daughter of Jay Gould, the railroad magnate, purchased the land and presented it to the National Board. Miss Dodge, Mary Billings French and four other board members contributed the cost of the building itself. The budget for equipment and furnishings was met by community Associations and National Board and staff members. With Miss Dodge, board members supervised every detail from the first architectural drawing to the planning of the service of dedication, held December 4, 1912. The best materials, expert workmanship, permanence and spacious serenity were their watchwords.

What in time would be called the YWCA's international work had begun in 1894 when the American Committee had joined with the YWCA of Great Britain to send Agnes Hill to India in response to an appeal from the YWCA of Madras for an experienced leader to help in its work with young women. This program of technical assistance, which by 1906 included thirteen workers on foreign assignments, was slowly expanded. It was directed by Harriet Taylor who had been general secretary for the American Committee, and of whom it was said by an irreverent colleague that "in any forty-eight hours she could have a hundred ideas, ninety-eight of which would be crazy, one workable, and one a stroke of sheer genius." In policy-making, Miss Dodge heavily supported those who believed that American secretaries should work under the supervision of the YWCA of the host country and not of the American YWCA, thereby establishing a sound philosophy that has admirably stood the test of time.

She was a member of the World's YWCA Committee and headed the American delegation to the World's meeting in Berlin in 1910. "I shall never forget the impression she made on me at once," wrote Lucy J. Tritton, then President of the World's YWCA, "as a rare example of a dominating personality, a born leader full of charm and sympathy, and above all, of her marvelous self-effacement." The night in Berlin when she addressed the audience of seven thousand people was, as her biographer puts it, "a majestic occasion. As she faced this vast, galleried assemblage, she was not too tall, too large. This was a proportionate setting for her; in such a perspective she was at ease."

Like the executive of an international business, she knew the whereabouts and current work of every staff member in the United States and overseas, with many of whom she kept in personal touch. The Riverdale postman told of delivering thirty or forty letters a day to her and taking away sixty or seventy, all written in her own hand. By her own records, in the period between 1907 and 1913, she wrote over 73,000 letters, in addition to hundreds of Christmas and Easter greetings.

A constant stream of YWCA visitors came in and out of the Madison Avenue house and Greystone in Riverdale, for weekends, luncheons, dinners, teatime talks. Meticulously punctual herself, she expected the same of others, although she always allowed three minutes for the difference in watches! Yet somehow, the secretaries testified, she created an unhurried atmosphere, full of cheerfulness and hope. Always they came away with new ideas, which she had drawn from them with skillful questions. She rarely discussed religion or spoke in conventionally religious terms. She personally believed in the Christian interpretation of life, but fully accepted others' differing views; further, Christianity, in her mind, was "a fact to be lived, not a system of opinions."

She was forthright in expressing the convictions she had gained in her years of experience, for example, that all members of an organization should participate in self-government, and that autonomy was important but so was the well-equipped, wisely-directed national office. Above all, she believed in long-range planning and the "think big" approach.

"We have to lay foundations not for one year or two years but for fifty years," she told the 1909 convention at Minneapolis.

"Our great movement is going to live for centuries. . . . We have to look at what thousands of girls will want or need in the future." Just as her father had once looked at world supply and world consumption of copper in making managerial decisions for the Phelps-Dodge copper interests, she now looked at the national and world needs of girls and women.

Her experience, unique for a woman of that day, enabled her to give a unique kind of leadership to women who lacked knowledge of organizational planning, who looked at budgets with the thrifty eye of the housewife, whose personal financial affairs were handled by husbands, male relatives or advisors. Over and over she told them—as she indeed had had to do with the men with whom she worked to establish the Teachers College—"Sometimes what seems to be an extravagance at the time proves in the long run to have been an economy."

The outbreak of World War I in the summer of 1914 was the beginning of the end for this magnificent woman. There is no other way to express it: it broke her heart. All over the continent of Europe she had friends who were dear to her. The work of the YWCA in European countries, as well as the international causes for which she had worked, were threatened. By nature she was a builder; her whole life had been so geared to the idea of constructive development that the wanton, senseless destructiveness of war was overwhelming to her. Her health was beginning to fail. Even at fifty, she had told a friend that she was "getting old"; now she was fifty-eight, and tired. Toward the end of December she suffered a stroke. On December 26, a group of foreign students had been invited to Greystone, for their annual holiday party with her. She had luncheon in her room, dressed for the party, but had to send her greetings and apologies to her guests. She died a few hours later.

In a short eight years this skilled arbitrator, this dreamer who seemed to be able to see into the future, this president who never lost sight of the details of broad policy, this generous contributor, had poured the wisdom of three decades of experience into the women's organization she believed in, and all over the globe YWCA secretaries were saying sadly, "She was my best friend." In the years to come, National Board members would time and time again, in the midst of discussing responsibilities that had fallen to them, pause to say, "If it had not been for Miss Dodge, we would not be ready for this."

CHAPTER THREE

~Mabel Cratty

Adventurer in Leadership

THE FIRST PERSON LISTED in Grace Dodge's appointment book for December 8, 1906, the first day after her election as the first president of the YWCA National Board, is "Miss Cratty." It was an entry destined to be repeated many hundreds of times in the next eight years. As general secretary of the National Board staff, a post which she entered a few months after the first convention of the new organization and in which she remained until her death in 1928, Mabel Cratty was a full partner in leadership of the common enterprise and a distinguished pioneer in the "new profession among women."

Her heritage was an ideal combination for one who must keep her feet on the ground yet look ahead and be a creative dreamer: she was one-quarter Scotch and three-quarters Irish. Born June 30, 1868, to Charles Campbell Cratty and Mary Thoburn Cratty in Bellaire, Ohio, she was the oldest of five children. Her Irish mother was a sister of Isabella Thoburn, the first unmarried woman missionary to go to another country from the United States, and of James Thoburn, for many years Bishop of the Methodist Episcopal Church in India. Her given name was made bearable to Mabel Cratty only because it combined those of her mother whom she dearly loved and her Aunt Isabella who was her childhood heroine. The two women were quite different in temperament, but young Mabel managed to incorporate into herself both her aunt's belief in the value of discipline and single-minded devotion to the task at hand, and her mother's gentle tolerance and humor.

The Cratty children were blessed with a happy, cheerful home, made quite special to them because of the presence of their paternal grandmother, a gentle, loving soul; Aunt Liddy, a former slave who had come into the Cratty home via the Underground Railroad; and a cousin, Mrs. Cratty's orphaned nephew, whom Mabel always called "my brother Lyle."

When in later years admiring staff members commented on how self-controlled she was, Mabel Cratty always chuckled. As a child, she said, she had had a "terrible temper." She vividly remembered throwing something at a neighborhood youngster and quaking with fear that she had committed murder. Though this incident turned out without consequence, there were others and finally her father took her aside. He confessed to her that he, too, had trouble controlling his temper, and they made a pact to help each other. And it was her father that instilled in her such a rigid sense of honesty that often in her life she had to remain silent rather than to say something she did not whole-heartedly mean.

When Mabel was seventeen, her father died and the family moved to Delaware, Ohio, the home of Ohio Wesleyan University. There were years of hard times for the family and to Mary Cratty, who had special names for each of her children, Mabel was her "tower of strength." The year before her father's death Mabel had graduated from Bellaire High School, and in 1890 she was a member of Phi Beta Kappa and an honors graduate from Ohio Wesleyan. Her first choice of career would have been to follow the Thoburns in India and, indeed, this would still have been her first choice sixteen years later when she was asked to be executive of the National Board staff. Both times her responsibility for her family ruled it out, a fact of life which she accepted serenely because, as her biographer explains, "she never seemed really to understand why people thought it made any difference where a person was working, or even what she was doing, as long as she was giving her best."

For fourteen years Miss Cratty followed the conventional pattern of the educated girl in the 1890s—she taught school. Twelve of those years were spent as Latin instructor, then principal, of the high school in Delaware, the town she always thought of as home. Once she wrote a friend who was going to visit there, "I envy you because you are to be in Delaware, every tree, brick and stone of which I love." She was fond of saying she learned about love while teaching school, as she found the only way to manage mischievous youngsters was to look beyond their behavior and to try to see them as their mothers saw them. "Love is *not* blind," she said. "It is only love that sees clearly."

She was persuaded to attend the Association training institute in the summer of 1902 by two college friends, Effie Price and Helen Barnes, who held staff positions with the American Committee of the YWCA at headquarters in Chicago and who had long hoped she might join them. For the next two years she served on the state committee in Ohio and in 1904 was called to the American Committee as associate general secretary. It was a wrench for her, but the committee members pleaded that they would not know where to turn if she could not accept.

Soon afterward came the crisis which precipitated the union of the two organizations and, following the convention of 1906, she and eleven other staff members moved from Chicago to the new headquarters in New York City.

"Several of us got together during the New York convention," recalls Theresa Wilbur Paist, who was then a member of the student staff, "and exchanged fears that the new board might not want our services. Of course, there was great discussion among us as to who would be chief. Harriet Taylor, our general secretary, made it clear that she wished to give full time to the Foreign Division. Some claimed we should secure a woman who had recognition as a great person, to give public evidence that we were a great new movement. It was good that Miss Cratty was chosen. What a team she and Miss Dodge made!"

It was with considerable trepidation that Miss Cratty accepted the appointment. "It's a very serious thing for a woman of my age [she was thirty-eight] to attempt a job that she has no assurance that she can carry successfully," she soberly told her colleagues. As she herself might say, she spent the next twenty-two years learning the job, and what she learned, she taught others. Thanks to her biographer, many helpful ideas expressed in her own words were preserved for succeeding generations.

The newly-transplanted staff lived at first in boarding houses near the headquarters office at 28th Street and Lexington Avenue. Later, Mabel Cratty, with Theresa Wilbur and Florence Simms, took an apartment near the Columbia University campus. Young Miss Wilbur, only a few years out of college, looked upon the new arrangement as just another dormitory, but Miss Cratty, who was both older and more domestic, insisted that this was a *home*. Abetted by Grace Dodge, who loaned them some splendid antique pieces, she scraped floors, painted second-hand furniture and sewed curtains and slipcovers to make it into a home that was the setting for Sunday night suppers that became famous among staff and their friends for good food and hilarity.

If she hadn't been a YWCA secretary, Mabel Cratty often said, she would have liked to be an interior decorator. Even her desk drawers at the office were resplendently lined with fitted pieces of rose-colored blotter which she bought herself, rejecting the somewhat ugly brown blotters provided by the organization. She loved color—pastels when she was younger, later after a visit to Czechoslovakia, the more vivid colors. She often chose a violet shade to wear, perhaps because it looked well with her gray-blue eyes and her hair which grayed early and was pure white before she was fifty.

The three housemates did their own housework, cooking and laundry. Miss Cratty enjoyed washing and ironing. It was a soothing change from work at the office, she said. Once the national secretary of the German YWCA stayed with them for several weeks on a "state" visit to the United States. "Now I know why you Americans are all so well dressed, compared with us Europeans," she finally commented, explaining that in her country, whatever her salary, a woman of professional status would always have to figure on paying for a maid.

It was a five-mile bus ride to work. Miss Cratty enjoyed the trip, partly because it gave her time to think, but mostly because she enjoyed the people who were her fellow passengers. Her favorite escape from cares and responsibilities was to go shopping in Woolworth's because she liked "that feeling of being among people."

She was a modest person, even shy, and in any given group, spoke up far less often than others. Yet what she said came from such thoughtful depths and was so well-expressed that it was both memorable and influential. She represented the YWCA on the National Social Work Council, the predecessor of today's National Social Welfare Assembly, members of which were dismayed at their loss when she died. Each was head of a national organization, and all were frank about their sense of personal dependence upon Miss Cratty and her good judgment. One of them said he had gone back over the stenotyped reports of their monthly meetings and had been amazed at how much less frequently than others she spoke, when she had been the one whose influence was strongest. "There was a world of meaning in her every sentence, every phrase, every word," he concluded, "and I myself find that I remember her exact words as I do those of few people."

Very early in National Board days Miss Cratty instituted what she called cabinet meetings, when the heads of departments would confer together. After one meeting, a staff member asked, noting how she had kept herself in the background, "Wherein is her leadership?"

"Perhaps some people never knew," recalls a member of that staff. "All of her leadership stemmed from the quality of herself and her life. She agreed perfectly with Miss Dodge's wish to have a group working together and no one person getting the credit or becoming the center of the organization. In fact, she had so much faith in what is now called the group process that I am sure we owe to her our tradition of holding large, widely-representative conventions. She believed all parts of the movement should be heard—and by each other."

Her faith in group thinking arose from her deep trust in people. Combined with her excellent judgment, her perception, her skill as a teacher and undergirded by her nurturing instinct, it made for topnotch performance as an administrator working closely with both laywomen and professionals.

"There was never a better teacher than Miss Cratty," wrote Emma Speer. "She taught us to look back to our grandmothers' lives, their duties and responsibilities, and to look forward to the future too, and to find the meaning of the changes in the world about us.... It was her habit to bring to the Executive Committee [of the National Board], when urgent routine things were disposed of, some significant fact, developing it month by month, as a composer develops a theme in a symphony, until the meaning of it had penetrated through and through and had become so truly a part of each individual's thinking that she could hardly remember when the idea was first given to her."

Both board and staff members thought of Mabel Cratty as an enabler. "I was a very young board member," says one, "and often I would be asked to do things I thought impossible for me. After a talk with her, I felt because of her trust in me, maybe I could do it. It was the trust—and that she was always available. Always the open door. That's very important."

"Her words stay with me to this day," says a staff member, now long retired. "Once she said 'Remember, my dear, praise, like blame, is like ice cream—soon gone!' It was exactly the right thing to say to a person like me." And another, who came to the national staff directly from college, says simply, "She brought me up."

Often her words combined briskness with humor. A staff member, back at the office after a meeting with the YMCA, sat at her desk looking forlornly at a book when Miss Cratty happened by. "The chairman was a minister," explained the young woman, "and you know I don't have as much religious background as some of the others have. I rushed back determined to brush up on theology, but this book—the writer's idea of what God is—well, I don't like it at all." "Did it ever occur to you" replied Miss Cratty, "that you don't have to believe everything you read?"

Another staff member was "blowing off steam" in Miss Cratty's office one day about a board member she felt was obstructing an important phase of program. After hearing her out, Miss Cratty said, eyes twinkling, "We might as well face it. Certain things will never be accomplished until certain people have gone to their reward!"

Her idea of an administrator was one who would be a resource, not a director; who was willing to suffer cheerfully for others' mistakes; who could keep in touch with details without getting lost in them; who liked people and had ability to work with them. Another necessary quality she implied in a talk about leadership: "Deliver us from being pompous!"

The status of women in American society was of great importance to her, but attaching importance to personal status was out of her ken. "Nothing needs less care than your position," she told students in the Training School, year after year, and when staff members complained about small offices, she proposed giving up her own office and had to be vetoed by the non-complainers. She applied the same philosophy to organizational status. During the hectic days of World War I, when the YWCA was one of the organizations asked by the government to give wartime service, she countered competitive attitudes in the YWCA family by saying, "It does not matter whether we get the credit for doing a thing. The only thing that matters is to have the right thing done." When the YMCA first instituted a program for women and girls, she bravely ran the risk of being labeled a "fighter for vested interests" because of her opposition to this development, although nothing could have been more alien to her character. The truth was, and this she was able to convey even to skeptics, that she feared that work for girls directed by men held the danger that "girls might not learn to stand on their own feet and might neither develop to their fullest stature nor give their best to society."

The greatest sacrifice of the administrator, in her view, was that the multiple demands of the job made it impossible to do everything on the level of her high standards. She cherished being able to talk and write "with a little artistry," as she told a board member. Nevertheless, many of her talks and writings that have been preserved to us are little masterpieces of wisdom with a timeless quality about them. Sometime in the 1920s, she ended a little talk about "ourselves and our religion" with a few sentences about what she thought it meant to "walk in the way of Jesus":

"Losing one's life in the process of pouring it forth steadily, continuously.

"Getting some kind of working attitude towards the whole problem of pain. Pain teaches nothing to the coward and everything to one who faces it. . . . It is the same with joy. Identify yourself with those who suffer and with those who rejoice.

"Keep, in these ways, close to life. Be an accessible person, not merely to a few chosen people, but to all kinds.

"Cease to live too much in the realm of ideas, and apply good will to life. This is the hardest of all, for we are apt to want God as a refuge *from* life.

"As a people, it is true that we have no great gift for religion. We are not the stuff of which good contemplatives are made. But we have some capacity for adventuring, for faring along even a thorny and hard-beset road."

To those who worked with her, her greatest artistry was in human relations. While she was a person of high standards for herself and her staff, she never asked or expected the impossible, her biographer tells us, illustrating with a story of a staff member who had failed in an assignment and, miserable, wrote Miss Cratty that she wished she could be "a workman that needeth not to be ashamed." "I don't know just what is meant by a workman who *needeth* not to be ashamed," replied her boss, "but deliver me from one who never *is* ashamed! Insufferable!"

She was deeply loyal to her staff and, cherishing their personal development, never hesitated to give them difficult assignments. She firmly believed that a position that was "along the line of least resistance" for a person did little to develop well-rounded qualities and once said, "I do not believe one should ever stay in a task after the struggle has gone out of it." However, she could identify completely with the person facing a difficult task. Once a staff member went to her on the eve of leaving for a new assignment and confessed she was afraid. "I am a poor person to come to," replied Mabel Cratty, "for I have walked in fear all my life."

She was slow to accept the need to shift people about when they had muffed a job. "We cannot be in the mood of easily sacrificing the person to the work," she said. When it became clear to her that a person could not succeed where she was, she insisted that the change be made in a way that would be helpful to the person, so that she could see the failure as a step in her development. In such a situation, she would not condone anything but complete honesty.

This first national staff were strong individualists—in some cases, one might even say prima donnas. "If ever there was a setup for anarchy!" exclaims a woman who knew them well. "But Miss Cratty liked them that way. She cherished their differences and told them so. She knew this was what generated the vitality that was so important at that stage. She would listen endlessly to the pros and cons of a situation, anxious only that no elements in it be overlooked. When a decision was reached, she would have had a part in it, but no more and no less than anyone else. When a staff member made a decision, she shared in its consequences, whether she had agreed with it or not. I never heard her say, 'If you had only done differently . . .' "

A fraternal delegate to one of the early conventions, who had worked closely with several staff members, commented on how in some organizations the staff seemed "cast in the same mold," but in the YWCA staff members were so different from each other that he wondered how they worked together. "But now that I have met Miss Cratty," he said, "I understand."

Distrust was the one thing she could not stand—"I do not mind the splutterings of irritation, and I can bear explosions of temper, but to have people distrust one another cuts me in two." She was cheerfully affectionate with her working companions and, when they were in real trouble, tenderly protective; but she was no coddler. Sensitiveness, she felt, "is a rare and beautiful quality if it is used to help you understand and interpret other people," but "it is a pity to waste and misuse it by thinking about yourself. There is no one so afflicting to work with as the person who is oversensitive." To those who thought their problems uniquely difficult, she would say, "Life is like that," and to those who suffered from wounded pride, "When one person has hurt another there is invariably the tendency of both to avoid each other. Don't give in to that. It is at just such a time that you need to seek out each other in order to restore normal relations."

The eight years of close work with Grace Dodge were to Miss Cratty "a long road of happy adventure." In a memorial volume about Miss Dodge, Miss Cratty wrote appreciatively of her president's hopefulness, sense of responsibility, "superb courage in the face of unexpected difficulties," true humility and "incredible patience" which, "being an impulsive person, she must have had to learn." For Miss Cratty and her apartment mates each working day began with an early morning telephone call from Miss Dodge. Much of their joint work was done at Miss Dodge's home and Miss Cratty became a favorite of the household staff, especially Dunlap the butler who fussed over her meals if he thought she looked tired or peaked. Peter, a cat, was the only family member excluded from this circle of mutual admiration. Because of Miss Cratty's lifelong aversion to cats, he was locked in the basement during her visits.

Together, these two women took a great part of the responsibility for the leadership which set the YWCA on a course that was to carry it far in two decades. One measure of its progress between 1906 and 1928 is the growth of the National Board staff from fourteen to one hundred and one, and of its budget from $136,000 to over $2 million. To Mabel Cratty, however, progress was not "more of what already is." For the YWCA, progress is, as she said in a long-remembered talk to students in the Training School, "the degree to which it is achieving the working together of ever-enlarging and more inclusive groups of women for ever-receding goals."

Leadership in such an enterprise, she said, "differs from some of the conventional uses of the word." The leader is not a "dominant person who goes ahead while others follow, who gives directions which others carry out." Leadership is "a result, a fruit, a grace of character, something earned, something always growing and never quite achieved.... We do not get it by seeking it.... Only as we have ceased to care for it does it begin to grow within us." The tests for the successful staff member, she said, were moral tests: willingness to face real issues of a particular job, willingness to take risks, willingness to get into a situation "where it is almost certain that we shall commit blunders," willingness to take responsibility for others' work when it may be "crude and unfinished," and "a constant passion for the development of our peers." A real leader must have faith in people and be able to instill that faith in others, and lest that sound too easy, she added, "It is an achievement to take people on faith. Sometimes we do it with our heads and not our hearts." Finally, she spoke about a sense of humor: "If we cannot laugh we make it very hard for those who have to work with us."

It was her Alma Mater that first called her an "international stateswoman," in awarding her an honorary Doctor of Laws degree in 1922. She had seen clearly, and conveyed to others, the meaning of the economic changes of the last century in the American home, the break in the continuity of human experience as young women exchanged work in the home for jobs in factories and shops. She saw the YWCA as an instrument forged to meet the need for spiritual values and to give women the inner strength these changes demanded. When war came, these concepts became global and more urgent, to her mind. She was one of twelve representatives of the YWCA of the U.S.A. on the World YWCA Council, which she saw, Emma Bailey Speer wrote, "as the heart of a great Christian woman's movement throughout the world, a movement that was taking one of the most significant facts of this generation, the change in the status of woman, and was directing it into a creative force. . . ." To Clarissa Spencer, a fellow student in the summer institute of 1902, who was general secretary of the World YWCA from 1904 to 1920, she was friend and counselor; and through the years, as she attended the seven meetings of the World YWCA that occurred during her incumbency and traveled extensively both on YWCA business and on vacations, she came to fill this role for countless others all over the world.

She died of pneumonia in New York City on February 27, 1928, a few months before she would have reached her sixtieth birthday. She would have been amused at the title of the editorial in *The New York Times* the next day; the editor had chosen to write of her and a well-known clergyman, Bishop Ethelbert Talbot, who had died the same day, under the heading "Two Bishops." "The status of women has changed during these twenty years," the editorial noted, "and one of the explanations of Miss Cratty's great success as an executive in all these changing phases has been her foresight in anticipating the direction which the social and economic development of women would take. Through the war and after, she was as a seer among her sisters. The secretaries she wisely guided now surround the globe."

CHAPTER FOUR

Emma Bailey Speer

'In the path of the winds and the tides'

IN THE CLOSING DAYS of the year 1914, the death of Grace Dodge dealt a cruel blow to the young national organization. With this strong hand of leadership lost to them, the small band of women devoted to the common ideal of Christian concerns faced each other with a seemingly unanswerable question: Who could fill Miss Dodge's place? They were unanimous in their answer: No one.

Agreement on this point opened the way to solution. Within days, the National Board divided the responsibilities which had been held by the president and created two jobs: president, and chairman of the executive committee. To fill the first they chose Mrs. Robert E. Speer; and for the second, Mrs. John French. Both were charter members of the National Board; both were in their early forties and had families of young children.

It could not have been easy for them to assume leadership responsibility, for while the direction had been charted, the paths ahead were unknown. They drew strength from the support of their fellow board members and from their mutual dedication to the YWCA and its potentialities for the future. Six weeks after her investiture in office, Mrs. Speer wrote a staff member, "Of course, if I let myself think of my own inadequacy,

I should give it all up—but Miss Dodge was always showing us that to a Christian the impossible is the thing to be done, and so I go on, with the things to be done, to be learned, new things to be thought through and related to the old."

Nearly four decades later she was to look back with her own mixture of humor and thankfulness on this time "when Mrs. John French and I became like Siamese twins," and how they had worked together for seventeen years "without the slightest jar or tension."

Tall, slim, dark in coloring, Mrs. Speer was a gay, eager, friendly, spirited person. Born May 15, 1872, in Pottstown, Pennsylvania, she was descended on her father's side from an English Quaker who came to William Penn's community in the 17th Century, and on her mother's side from Dutch and Scotch Presbyterian families. One of the latter strain, known in Pennsylvania as the "fighting parson," is said to have beseeched the Lord to give victory to the Americans in the Revolution, but added, "If Thou art unwilling by Thy divine grace to assist us, do Thou'st stand aside and let us fight it out."

Her father, Charles Bailey, was an ironmaster, as his father had been. Shortly after Emma was born, he moved his family to Harrisburg where he became president of the Central Iron Works and a leading citizen. Although he was expelled from his Quaker meeting for marrying a Presbyterian, he breathed Quaker custom and philosophy into the lives of his family. During her years as president of the National Board, Mrs. Speer once sent a Christmas card showing herself at age seven in a Quaker costume and bearing the message: "When we were very young, one of us looked like this. No longer a little Friend but just an old friend, she sends her love at Christmas."

Her mother, Emma Harriet Doll Bailey, was a distinct and powerful personality, endowed with both beauty and executive ability. For years she taught a large Bible class of men in their church in Harrisburg, and all her life was active in the work of the Presbyterian women's home missions. And always adventurous, she went off to Alaska at age seventy-three to inspect the Sheldon Jackson Mission.

Emma was the youngest of five children and the only girl. Her brothers, two to fifteen years older, made her the darling of them all and insisted, when the time came, that she have as good an education as they had at Yale. Until she was sixteen she was educated at home by a governess; then she went to a preparatory school and, in 1890, enrolled in the fifth class of Bryn Mawr College where "that radical young woman," M. Carey Thomas, was dean. Although romance and marriage interrupted Emma Bailey's college career, Bryn Mawr thought of her as one of its distinguished daughters and at its seventy-fifth anniversary awarded her a citation for "vision and faith in a life of great service."

In the spring of Emma's freshman year, Grace Dodge came to Bryn Mawr to talk about the Working Girls Societies and made an unforgettable impression on the nineteen-year-old student who would one day succeed Miss Dodge as president of the YWCA's National Board. "She was a leader to follow through thick and thin," she wrote once in a reminiscent mood.

That summer she was one of the first two women students to attend the annual YMCA student conference at Northfield Seminary in Massachusetts. She and the young Bible instructor, Robert E. Speer, were very drawn to each other. The following winter she invited him to speak to the Bryn Mawr students, and before the end of the year they were engaged. In the spring of 1893 when he was twenty-five and she not yet twenty-one, she left college and they were married.

Robert Speer had been brought up in a family which came of old American stock—a mixture of English, Scotch, Irish and Swiss. His father, a lawyer by profession, was leader of the Democratic party in Pennsylvania and served as Representative in Congress for two terms in the early 1870s. A handsome, brilliant man, he was a great platform speaker and a devout Christian. Robert was one of a family of five children, and was only nine when his mother died. He graduated from Phillips Academy and Princeton (Class of 1889), where he was an outstanding football player and won *magna cum laude* standing. He had intended to enter law, but midway in his Princeton years had been influenced by a leader in the student volunteer movement to go into foreign missions. While preparing for this calling at Princeton Theological Seminary, he was invited to become Secretary of the Board of Foreign Missions of the Presbyterian Church, a post which he entered in 1891 and in which he remained until retirement.

For the first three years of their marriage, the Speers lived in Elizabeth, New Jersey, and Mrs. Speer accompanied her husband on the trips he took in the line of duty. In the fall of 1896 they began a trip around the world to visit mission stations. In Persia, Emma Speer's expertness as a horsewoman, acquired on her father's Pennsylvania farm, came in handy.

"We have accomplished the long horseback journey from Tabriz to Hamadan," she wrote her mother in early November, 1896. "Most caravans take seventeen days but we did it in eleven and a half, getting up at three or four and starting out in the moonlight about five. It is a great mistake to think that Persia is a warm country. The climate is just about like ours and you know what it is like at five o'clock on a November morning at home. My horse is a jewel. He is light gray, strong and well-formed and has absolutely perfect gaits, a fast walk, smooth pace and easiest canter imaginable. We call him 'The Country Gentleman.' Rob's horse, a darker gray and not so pretty nor so easy, is 'The Plodding Farmer.' "

Three weeks later she wrote in great distress to say Dr. Speer had been taken ill. "Here we are twenty-four days from the nearest railroad . . . a place where we cannot send or receive cablegrams and from which it takes six weeks for a letter to reach

New York. High mountains (14,000 ft.) around us, the winter storms just beginning, just eleven English-speaking people among 80,000 inhabitants—and Rob, who has never been ill since I have known him, who hardly ever was even tired, has typhoid fever!"

The twenty-four-year-old Emma Speer showed the practicality and spiritual strength which were to be marks of her mature years:

"I have had to sit down and face my situation while Rob was asleep. Several things stood out very clearly: 1. If I had any good stuff in me, now was the time to show it. 2. God would take care of us here just as well as in New York and that His way is always loving, no matter how hard it might seem. 3. I am thankful to be here rather than in some little hole on the way to Baghdad [as they would have been according to earlier plans]. 4. I have confidence in our doctor, who is a medical missionary of twenty years standing in Persia."

After two months Dr. Speer was sufficiently recovered to resume the journey, and during the summer of 1897 they returned to New Jersey and bought a house in Englewood, then a small community on the edge of the wooded Palisades. Here, between 1898 and 1910, their five children were born; and for thirty years, they enjoyed happy friendships with neighboring young families, their Shakespeare Club, their church, and most of all their big house, cheerfully overrun with big and small Speers, returned Presbyterian missionaries and staff and board members of the YWCA.

At the request of Emma Bailey and the other woman student who went to the Northfield conference in 1891, a conference for women students had been arranged in 1892, led by staff members of the student division of the American Committee, YWCA. They "quickened and confirmed the impression Miss Dodge had made," Mrs. Speer once wrote, "that there were things important and vitally interesting to be done for and with girls in our changing world." Soon afterward she joined the American Committee, feeling "a little out of my element among the dignified matrons." She worked on the student committee, became its chairman, and in due course was appointed to the Joint Committee which paved the way for the first convention of the united organization. It was then, she later said, that "my education began in earnest!"

"How Emma worked when she was chairman of the student committee!" recalls Theresa Paist. "She had children and babies, and she was a commuter—the hard kind of commuting, where you walked to the station, took a train down the river, went across on a ferry and then took a trolley to the YWCA."

Mrs. Paist, then Theresa Wilbur and a student staff member, as well as many other YWCA folk often had occasion to make the trip in reverse order, and the Speer children came to know them well. "We were taught to have great respect for the professional staff," testifies a daughter, recalling some of the colorful people who had great stories to tell. Mrs. Speer liked to have these visitors join in family life, and today there are those who remember helping a young Speer mop up spilled egg at the breakfast table and hearing Mrs. Speer read the *Jungle Tales* to the little ones at bedtime. It was a rare treat, too, to see the serious Dr. Speer in the bosom of his family, carrying on lively conversations with the children, reading O. Henry stories aloud, teasing his wife. (Once when she was out of sorts at the dinner table, he observed, "I see we have snapdragons on the table tonight.")

He thought she was inclined to be impulsive, and so she was; but he, like the YWCA, learned that when she made what appeared to be a quick decision, saying comfortingly, "Now, this is going to be a good idea," it usually was, and he went along with it. In the Speer family annals the most famous example is her on-first-sight purchase of Rockledge, their house in Lakeville, Connecticut, which she saw by happenstance on her way to visit her son in prep school. Dr. Speer loved it at once, too, and it served them as summer home and retirement home and then her own home for the fifteen years between his death and hers.

In Emma Speer, the YWCA had a true 20th Century woman leader. Intelligent and educated, she enjoyed using her brain and education. Her tastes were eclectic and wide-ranging, and she possessed both literary appreciation and skill. She loved Kipling and was especially interested in Gaelic literature. She had no trace of the Lady Bountiful which so strongly flavored the social reforms of the late 19th Century. She had a great sense of the movement of history and was vocal about her "profound belief in the as yet unrealized possibilities of women in national and world life which it was the purpose of the YWCA to develop and nourish," as it was put by Anna Rice, the National Board's second general secretary.

"In 1906," wrote Mrs. Speer later in her career, "the life of women was no longer to be lived in quiet backwaters or hidden harbors. It was moving swiftly out to sea, to be in the path of all the winds and tides, all the hurricanes and thunderclouds that were already making the horizon dark." She shared Grace Dodge's enthusiasm for the "new profession among women"— the YWCA secretaryships—for, as she put it, "Only trained pilots could take a ship out into such weather—women who saw beneath the surface and turned dream into reality." Then and later, the Training School was to her "the chief asset of the young national organization." She appreciated deeply those among the board members who, as she wrote of one of them, "saw the meaning of the trends of her day" and possessed "the graciousness of true Christians in being open-minded to new methods for a new day." It was to women like this, she felt, that the YWCA owed its existence.

Not one to confine expression of her personal convictions to one segment of her life, she also talked about these matters at home, which influenced the attitudes of her children and probably her husband. "My father always believed in what women could do," says their daughter, "and during his regime the women's Board of Missions moved from an auxiliary to a genuine part of mission work. Though not a crusader about it, he was ready for women to have much more of a place in the church than they even do today."

To women like Mrs. Speer, it was logical to lend support to the woman-suffrage movement, since they were interested in helping women achieve stature and status. Although the YWCA took no formal action either in support or opposition, many of the staff were deeply involved in the movement. Regardless of where their sympathies lay, most National Board members did not approve of demonstrations, but Mrs. Speer joined the YWCA contingent in one of the large suffragists' parades that took place in New York City.

When the YWCA's concern for its own members who were underpaid and overworked industrial workers led the organization, beginning in 1911, into social action and later plunged it into the midst of the searing controversy of the postwar period concerning the labor movement, she gave wholehearted encouragement.

"She would go to call on husbands of board members—and mind you, lots of our board were downright afraid of their husbands—and argue the eight-hour day to beat the band," a former staff member recalls. "It was anathema to some of them, but more often than not, she came back with a good-sized check in her pocket for YWCA industrial work. I remember one large contributor saying of her and two other women who were good money-raisers, 'That triumvirate! I've never seen their like. You have to hang onto your pocket with both hands. They have the greatest way of getting around you.'"

Straightforward, never hedging or hesitating on what she thought, she rejoiced in having women of the same ilk to work with. A staff member who worked closely with the Executive Committee recalls, "They weren't afraid of man nor beast, and certainly not afraid to differ. They could get quite heated in their discussions. I can hear them now: 'But *Emma!*' when she would get going in that half-inspired, half-impulsive way of hers."

Two years after Emma Speer and Mary French embarked on their career as "Siamese twins," the United States entered World War I, and the YWCA became the one women's organization of the seven whose help the government enlisted. After a decade of modest annual budgets, the board was suddenly confronted with the responsibility of administering $4 million in one year. Swamped with volunteers, they lived through an explosive period of expansion, which moved them from what one charter board member calls "a one-horse operation" to an important national organization.

Recounting these and other events during Mrs. Speer's presidency, Theresa Paist said, following Mrs. Speer's death, "How did she do it? If you could tell someone how to be a great leader in outline form, it would be very nice. I only know some of the elements that went into it. She took her own personal responsibilities very seriously. Her life was a unit. She was a woman of prayer and a woman of great courtesy. I remember Mary French saying 'Emma is such a lady.' And she was. Her hair somehow stayed in order. She could wear gloves and not be bothered by it. Her clothes stayed with her. She lived an orderly life. She had respect for learning and was a great reader. She believed in words as part of the way you communicate, and she expressed herself well both in speaking and writing."

Then she recalled a time after Mrs. Speer had retired from the presidency when, during a convention discussion, "we were very low and she came in to talk to us." The issue of the moment was long forgotten, she said, but she still remembered vividly how Mrs. Speer "gave us courage when we were bewildered, because she could persuade us to remember the integrity of the universe and the fact that there were still laws on which we could count."

Emma Speer died at the home of her daughter in Bryn Mawr, on December 23, 1947, at the age of eighty-five, and to quote part of her own favorite sentence from *Pilgrim's Progress,* "All the trumpets sounded for her on the other side."

CHAPTER FIVE

Mary Billings French

'God gave us hills and strength for climbing'

THE BLOOD of American pioneers flowed through the veins of Mary Montague Billings and she used her heritage of courage well. Her birthplace and childhood home was in the hills of Vermont, in one of the most beautiful old towns of New England, and she valued and nourished her sense of belonging there, returning to spend part of each year as long as she lived. Wherever she went, she carried a great love and appreciation of nature, first learned in the Vermont countryside. The deeply religious faith of her family, almost Puritan in quality, remained with her and matured in her through the years of responsibility and world-shaking change.

Her New England parents had married after a whirlwind romance and lived first in California, where Frederick Billings, fresh out of college, hung up the first lawyer's shingle in San Francisco and became one of the founders of the Northern Pacific Railroad. Mary was born March 5, 1869, in Woodstock, Vermont, near her father's boyhood home. She was one of seven children, which may explain the ease and humor with which she adapted to groups of which she was a part later in life.

Rich in historical distinctions such as having four churches whose bells were cast by Paul Revere, Woodstock was the home of distinguished scholars and a leading publishing center. The route on the railroad spur line which connected it with White River Junction sixteen miles away was considered one of the most scenic in the East. Halfway between the two towns the railroad crossed the Queechee Gorge by a bridge one hundred and sixty-five feet above the narrow, turbulent Ottauqueechee river.

The flavor of life in the Vermont town stayed with Mary forever and accounted for some delightful references in the talks she gave at the YWCA National Board. Stock-taking at annual meeting reminded her of the annual visit she and her brothers and sisters made to their aunts' brick house on Woodstock's village green, where "we were stood up against the wall, a book placed on our heads and we were measured, to keep a record of our growth from year to year." At Thanksgiving time she recalled the Harvest Festivals "in the little white meeting houses of Vermont when pumpkins, squash, apples, potatoes, turnips, carrots, corn and wheat were used as decorations. How their luscious colors and varied shapes stood out against those bare walls ... like a touch of sunny Italy in a little New England village on the very threshold of a long cold winter." Springtime brought memories of riding with her brothers and sisters over the crunching frozen snow in an ox-cart to watch the men at work when the sap in the maple trees began to run; and how "the woods where we went were not all maples, there were hemlocks making dark shadows in the snow, and white birches almost melting away into the wintry landscape, and beech trees with their grey and mottled trunks." The people, too, came back to her. In a little talk on courtesy, she told of driving with a party of teenagers along the banks of the river to visit "a beautiful old lady who seemed to me to personify the very spirit of courtesy," and recalled that as the young people talked with her, "unconsciously our manners became more gracious, our voices less strident and our English purer."

As a girl, Mary Billings had many of the accepted female ac-
complishments of the day; for example, she was a water colorist
of some talent. She was a robustly healthy young woman, ener-
getic, quick-moving and venturesome. She loved to ride (alter-
nating from a right sidesaddle to a left one, so that one leg would
not grow longer than the other!) and became a golfer when the
game was still not quite thought of as a woman's pastime. Once,
out of sheer exuberance, she persuaded a railroad engineer to let
her ride the cowcatcher of his engine over the sixteen-mile route
from White River Junction. The real thrill, of course, was cross-
ing the Queechee Gorge. Gleefully, she came home to recount
her adventure to her mother. "The next time I ride the cowcatcher," she added, "I think I'll wear a duster." The horrified
Mrs. Billings drew herself up and replied, "There will be no next
time, Mary."

Mary was the first person in Woodstock to own and drive an
automobile. Everywhere, in those first days of the horseless carriage, horse owners were protesting that the machines were
frightening the horses and causing accidents. One day Mary
took a beau for a ride and, after passing a horse and buggy, she
looked back and exclaimed, "Look! The horse is rearing and
going off the road." Quietly, her swain replied, "So are we, Mary."
Shortly after this incident she took a thoughtful and practical
action: she advertised in the local newspaper that, with the per-
mission of the owner of a nearby race track, she would drive her
car around the course for several stated hours each week—and
anyone who wished to could bring his horse and buggy and drive
around with her to accustom the horse to being on the road with
the machine.

When Mary Billings became interested in the YWCA before
the turn of the century, she had graduated from Miss Porter's
School in Connecticut, was at home in the social circles of New
York City where the family lived part of each year, and had
traveled abroad fairly extensively. Her mother had worked for

some time with the American Committee of the YWCA and was one of the donors of funds to open a World's YWCA office in London in 1894. Mary became a member of the American Committee and was appointed to the committee guiding student work. By 1905, she was a seasoned volunteer. A dedicated member of the working committee that brought the new national organization into being, she was elected a charter member of the National Board at the famous convention in New York City in December, 1906.

The following year she married John French, also of a Woodstock family, and in the next years had a son and two daughters. As Mr. French was a New York lawyer, the family divided their time between houses in the city and in Greenwich, Connecticut. Mary French was continuously involved in the work of the National Board; in the forty-five years of her membership on it, she served eighteen years as chairman of the Executive Committee and held membership on nearly every other committee there was. She traveled back and forth from Greenwich to the YWCA, enjoying the trip which in those days was accomplished by train and trolley. Even during her pregnancies, she maintained that while commuters might grumble, she found the trip enjoyable.

For several years of Grace Dodge's presidency, Mary French worked on the major project of making a dream come true: the establishment of the national headquarters office. With Miss Dodge and four other women, she contributed the money required for the building; and with them she pored over the blueprints and worked with the architects.

At home, she rose early and saw to it that each day began with family prayers. Always punctual herself, she made sure the rest of the family was right on time, whether it be to leave for a European trip or for a family picnic. In Greenwich and Woodstock, she spent part of each day out of doors. For many years her companion on nature walks was her bloodhound, Wolfie. One of the saddest days of her life was the day Wolfie had to be destroyed because he had developed unfriendly habits and tried to bite people who were strange to him.

Her infectious laugh rang through the French home. She seemed to find great humor in small everyday happenings. She was slow to anger and well-controlled. Her daughters, Mary and Elizabeth, do not remember her uttering a word in anger, but they do remember "that steely look Mother got that was more effective than any words!"

She entertained often and it was written of her that "she had a gift for friendship which made her hospitality a joy." A visitor was aware that the reason she had such extraordinary cooperation from her household staff was because they were her friends. The warmth and simplicity with which she welcomed guests to her home made them realize that she was genuinely interested in them.

Mary French always regretted that she hadn't gone to college. Once she was bidden to a party where guests were to come dressed to represent "your suppressed desire." Other women came dressed for opera roles or as tango dancers. Mrs. French appeared in a borrowed academic cap and gown. Later, she won her own cap and gown when she was awarded an honorary Master of Arts degree by Middlebury College, Vermont. She had the curiosity and persistence of the good student and thorough researcher. For a Thanksgiving talk to the National Board and staff, which she titled "An Adventure of Youth," she had gone back to the records of the Pilgrims to document a little-known fact about those first New Englanders:

"How young those Pilgrims were!" she said. "Of the 102 persons who came over in the Mayflower, 39 were under twenty-one years of age. Bradford, the great heart of the group, was exactly thirty-one. John Alden was twenty-one. Only two of the entire group were over fifty and only nine over forty. Veritably, this was an adventure of youth."

She belonged to a literary group which precisely suited her. The members prepared "mystery papers," so called because they were read anonymously, after which club members guessed the name of the author. For her own mystery papers, she most often did research about some aspect of nature which interested her and linked it to a philosophical idea.

Like so many of her early YWCA colleagues, she was tall— five feet, nine inches. She was a brunette, with inquiring, humorous gray eyes, and her features were bold and striking. Even if we had no record to prove it, we should know from Mary French's portrait that she had a rich inner life, which she cultivated and nourished. Writing each evening in a little red notebook, which she did for twenty-five years, was her practical answer to a perennial problem of a woman: how to preserve some small area of life, away from the duties of a wife, mother, homemaker, community volunteer, that is strictly her own.

It was part of her daily routine to record in the notebooks those expressive words, phrases, thoughts and ideas she felt were worth preserving. From the Bible, Shakespeare and other poets, from newspapers and magazines and new books she had been reading, from letters and greetings from friends, from church and YWCA publications and minutes of committee meetings, carefully she wrote into her notebooks the sentences and paragraphs that had especial meaning for her. It was to the notebooks she turned when she was preparing a talk, and often she would add to these pages parts of her talks for future reference. Sometimes she shared the day's treasure with family members or friends, but essentially her choices represented the feelings and ideas that meant most to her.

In *Thoughts and Meditations,* a volume of selections from her notebooks, published by her daughter Mary after her death, one sees in capsule form what those feelings and ideas were—her joy in nature and the changing seasons, and those human qualities she so admired: patience, courtesy, humor, serenity, sensitiveness; and the significance of all experience to those of deep faith and Christian love.

She was a steadfast woman. Her interest and concern for the YWCA grew and deepened with the years, as she matured from the young girl who became interested in the student work to the busy matron who valiantly took on the chairmanship of the National Board's Executive Committee, and then to the seasoned woman of middle years who carried that job, along with many others, through the first crucial decades of the organization's life. She took a particular interest in the YWCA's international work, in both world wars and the postwar periods. During World War II, when headquarters of the World's YWCA was moved temporarily to Washington and North American women were asked to act as proxy for European members of the Executive Committee, Mrs. French took this responsibility in behalf of Fru Elsa Cedergren of Sweden.

Only once did Mrs. French refuse a responsibility she was asked to take. After eighteen years of chairing the Executive Committee, she was asked to allow her name to be proposed as president of the National Board. She declined because she wished to have more free time to spend with her husband. A few years after his death, although she herself was approaching seventy, the invitation was again extended and this time she agreed, and served for two years.

The years of World War I and it dizzying aftermath were years of hard decisions for the National Board. As a presiding officer or committee member, Mary French could always be counted on for excellent judgment, wisdom and great integrity. An independent thinker, she did not hesitate to express her difference from others' opinion. At the same time, she took a thoughtful approach to problems and was unwilling to make snap judgments. "Let us think about it," she would say when a new idea was proposed, "and then let's talk about it again." It was said of her that one of her secrets was in using the Quaker method of finding "the sense of the meeting" buried beneath the differences, and so "she never left behind divided or antagonistic factions."

In the countless times she was called upon to open and set the tone for a meeting, she showed herself to be well aware of the turmoil of the times and quietly shared her distress, her courage and her faith. "In this distracted and anxious world of ours," she would begin, or "Amid these days of destruction and devastation," giving voice to the universal concern of her listeners, and then would go on to talk about the eternal values and the constant, reassuring manifestation of God's love. In September, 1938, when world attention was riveted on the fateful Munich Conference, Mrs. French spoke at a meeting of the National Board and staff with foreign guests.

"Under the extreme tension of these past days," she said, "we, too, are bewildered and benumbed and not knowing what the next hour may bring forth, we find it hard to concentrate on anything. God grant that His way may be revealed to us as we counsel together, that we may be given wisdom and strength for the responsibilities entrusted to us . . . and courage to make bold decisions if they be in line with the guidance of the Holy Spirit."

During happier days, ten years earlier, she reported to the National Board on the National Convention of the YWCA at Sacramento, showing her sensitivity to the "sense of the meeting."

"One morning we woke up to find ourselves on a divide high up between mountains," she said, in describing her trip west, "with snow on either side, yet below and to the west of us a veritable garden, fruit trees, flowers and running streams. Life was there. Life in abundance. And life seemed to me to throb throughout the convention . . . I have been wondering just what it was that gave this impression of vitality. Could it have been because the proportion of youth to the whole was greater than at previous conventions? Or because youth more generally shared responsibilities? Or because those who were older evidenced a greater willingness to put themselves in youth's place? Or was it because, perhaps as never before, we were conscious of the living spiritual presence of a great cloud of witnesses?"

In her judgment of persons and ideas, Mary French had what one devoted friend on the staff called "sympathetic appreciation of the viewpoint of persons whose life experiences were utterly different from her own." In the 1920s when the Retirement Fund for YWCA secretaries was being set up, she worked longer hours and took on the task of persuading some more doubtful members of the board that this was a right step to take. She also wrote a firm letter to New York's Governor Alfred E. Smith, asking him not to delay signing the Act of Incorporation of the Fund.

It fell to her lot to preside at a reception for Queen Marie of Romania, who visited the headquarters building during her state visit to the United States in the mid-20s. As she and a staff member waited for the royal entourage to arrive, they compared notes about the proper way to greet the Queen. "If we were in her country," said Mrs. French, "of course we'd curtsy. But since she's in ours, perhaps the best thing to do is just be ourselves." When the Queen arrived, they shook hands with her, American fashion, and all went well.

Mrs. French was a devout Presbyterian, but her "appreciation of other points of view" made her very interested in the ecumenical movement. She was for years a devoted member of the National Conference of Christians and Jews and carried responsibility for the YWCA's work with the National Council of Churches in the United States and the World Council of Churches, once representing the YWCA at a world meeting of the latter.

After her death in the summer of 1951 in Hanover, New Hampshire, amid her beloved New England mountains, a memorial service was held at the headquarters building. The details of the forty-five years of service given by Mary Billings French to the National Board were recalled, and various board and staff members who had served with her spoke of their memories of her. A particularly fitting memorial came from one staff member: "She combined depth of insight into spiritual things, practical wisdom in mundane affairs, and a certain gaiety of temperament which made her not only a tower of strength but also an altogether charming companion."

Today, her two daughters, Mrs. Laurance S. Rockefeller and Mrs. Ethan Allen Hitchcock, have followed in their mother's footsteps as hard-working and devoted members of the National Board. They and other members who knew Mrs. French or who have read her writings find inspiration in her hopes for women and the YWCA which she expressed so well in a Thanksgiving talk in 1927:

"As I repeat the line 'God gave us hills to climb and strength for climbing,' I wonder if we believe that to have hills to climb is a cause for thanksgiving. If we do, our hearts should be filled with gratitude today for there are hills and mountains aplenty in the path that lies before the YWCA and I believe some of these hills have never before been scaled.

"We can be thankful that women are having increasing opportunities not only to oil the wheels of life that they may run more smoothly up the steep grades ahead, but that they are becoming more of a factor, if they will, in determining the direction in which the wheels of life shall move.

"Let us be thankful, too, that in these days of experimentation and group research, the YWCA is trying out its belief that fellowship practiced by women of different classes and races the world over is leading to discoveries of good will and understanding that will change hatred and suspicion into friendship and love."

CHAPTER SIX

*U*era Scott Cushman

Watcher of the Skies

AT MID-CENTURY, looking back on that shocking summer when World War I broke out, the YWCA's Emma Speer said, "Those of you who are so much younger and have lived always in a broken and torn world can hardly realize what it was to us to see our stable world falling to pieces in 1914, and to know it would never come back." Though some people clung to the belief that it could and would come back, she went on to say, the women leaders who saw the YWCA through those war years knew it could not. Moreover, they "saw what could be done with the new world we were moving into . . . saw it still as God's world with roads ahead, passable but unsafe," and most important, "knew that girls and women were the chief unused resource of that world."

One of those leaders was Vera Cushman, who as chairman of the War Work Council, created by the National Board in May, 1917, shared duty with Helen Davis, the council's executive, at the helm of a vast enterprise.

That spring, Mrs. Cushman was approaching her forty-first birthday. For half of her life she had loved and worked for the YWCA. Tall and poised, she had been a golden-haired, violet-eyed beauty in her youth. In maturity, she was lovelier than ever, for she was a happy, vital, intelligent woman. Her extraordinary charm won the admiration of men and women alike. She was a delight to work with because, said one of her YWCA associates, "her bubbling, irrepressible humor never deserted her, yet it never displaced deep gravity when the occasion called for it."

Born September 19, 1876, into a well-to-do, socially-prominent Illinois family, Vera Scott was brought up by deeply religious parents who had a strong feeling for foreign missions. One of her two brothers, Reverend George T. Scott, became assistant to Dr. Robert E. Speer in the foreign missions work of the Presbyterian Church and went on to direct the Church's Foreign Department for two decades.

Emma Speer, who knew the Scott family well, has said that Vera's mother was "a woman of vision and faith. She had what we later came to call 'the planetary mind,' for her vision was of the whole world won to the love of God." From babyhood on, Mrs. Speer said, Vera "was trained to think first of others' comfort, well-being and pleasure, and of creating around her an atmosphere of pleasantness and good cheer. She was taught to regard thoughtfulness of others as an essential part of Christian character and courtesy."

At Smith College, where she graduated in 1898, Vera Scott worked hard in student activities. In later life she spoke gratefully of "the marvelous developing experience" of her college years, and was always active in alumnae affairs. When she was a sophomore, she attended the Northfield summer conference, where she met Harriet Taylor and Bertha Condé, staff members of the YWCA's American Committee in Chicago. From then on she was a YWCA enthusiast and served as president of the student Association at Smith. "I can see her now," wrote a college friend many years later, "leading the Smith delegation across the Northfield campus. She wore mauve linen and her hair was a golden halo. Even if her words had not been so wise and inspiring, her beauty and radiant smile could hold you."

After graduation Vera Scott continued her interest in the American Committee's student work. She was appointed to the Joint Committee whose efforts led to creation of a united, national YWCA, and was elected a charter member of the National Board.

In 1901 she had married a New Yorker, James Cushman. "When he brought her home, she just took New York society by storm," recalls an old friend. Mr. Cushman, a paper manufacturer and real estate developer (he is credited with designing and building the New York residence hotels, the Allerton Houses), shared his young wife's discriminating interests. From the beginning of their marriage, only those friends whom they found interesting and worthwhile were entertained at the old brownstone house in the East 90s where they first lived and the splendid Fifth Avenue mansion which was their home later. Always among their guests were young people, with whom they had such affinity that their close friends mourned their never having had children of their own.

She was a famous hostess. "She loved to invite different kinds of people and mix them up," says a friend who was one of her favorite young people. "Sometimes at her parties no one would have met any of the other guests before. She had a knack of bringing people together who had something in common and getting them started. I should know! I was engaged to my husband before I knew she had already picked him for me when she introduced us!"

Vera Cushman's mature leadership qualities were brought into full play when Grace Dodge appointed her to the Metropolitan Provisional Committee, which brought all YWCA work in New York City under one board of directors. It was no small task; seven autonomous programs, such as residences, activities centers and an International Institute, were involved, and there was strong feeling both for and against having a loose federation of the programs rather than a centralized directorship body.

"Mrs. Cushman had great ability to sense a need, vision to see how best it could be met, and ability to make that vision a reality," said a National Board member who knew much about the delicate negotiations which led to the New York City YWCA merger in May, 1912. "Some people have one or two of those qualities but she had all of them. She truly was concerned that people 'might have life and have it more abundantly.' Organization concerned her only as a means to that end."

The newly-united city Association must have appreciated this philosophy, for it chose Vera Cushman for its first president. As such, she served as vice-chairman of the "Whirlwind Campaign," a joint effort with the YMCA of New York City in November, 1913, to raise money for new buildings for both organizations. In campaign annals it is famous, for the goal of $4 million was reached in fourteen days.

When representatives of the national YWCA were called to Washington in the spring of 1917, shortly after the United States had entered the war, to consult with government officials about what the organization was prepared to do in the critical days ahead, they went proudly—and with good reason. Eleven years before they had established a national organization, a revolutionary move for a day when the United States was still highly sectionalized in feeling; now there was YWCA work in every state of the nation. International organizational ties were even more unusual, but there were forty-seven trained American secretaries at work in the YWCAs of five foreign countries, and the YWCA of the U.S.A. was one of the mainstays of the World's YWCA.

They had proved to themselves, and whoever else cared to observe it, that women could raise money and administer budgets. Programs in full swing in paid-for buildings in more than two hundred cities and the substantial headquarters building in New York City testified to that. Scores of secretaries had graduated from the Training School and fanned out over the country, bringing specialized services in physical education, religious education, employment, recreation, case work, residence and room registry to the women and girls of American communities. Programs for and with adolescent girls, women industrial workers, Negro women and girls, and foreign-born and second-generation Americans had begun. At the Panama-Pacific International Exposition in San Francisco in 1915, the national organization had maintained a headquarters and club house for service to women visitors. In the summer of 1916, because of concentration of troops on the Mexican border, it had begun special work for girls in cooperation with city Associations in Texas and Arizona.

Although in 1917 they were still legally a "minority group," women had found in the YWCA an opportunity to put their talents, education and ideas to work in a way that satisfied their religious motivation, their concern for the needs of women and girls, and their own need for self-fulfillment. In so doing, they had created a respected, well-established, useful addition to the national community.

Almost immediately after the Washington talks, the YWCA was designated by the government as one of the seven official war service organizations. The group also included the American Library Association, the Federal Council of Churches of Christ in America, the Jewish Welfare Board, the National Catholic War Council, the Salvation Army and the YMCA. All the agencies participated in the united war work campaigns, but each of them planned its program independently, subject to instructions received directly from the government.

Vera Cushman was, as Emma Speer was to phrase it, "the logical choice" for chairman of the YWCA's war work. She was practical, an actionist, a good organizer, and a sophisticated, warm and friendly woman who was at home wherever she went. Not only was she attractive to men, but she could meet them on a par and conduct business with them confidently. She was well-traveled and was as at home in Europe as she was in her own country. "It is impossible to exaggerate what we owe her and the group who worked with her in those creative years," wrote Mrs. Speer. "We were literally swamped with money and volunteers and had to steer a steep course between doing too little and taking on too much."

Early in the summer of 1917 a friend of the Cushmans, the commanding officer at the Army camp at Plattsburgh, New York, appealed to the new War Work Council chairman, saying he had no suitable place for his men to meet their womenfolk. Mrs. Speer has described Mrs. Cushman's response: "She saw right away what might be done and where it would lead. A good friend of the YWCA gave $10,000, and in two weeks the house was built and furnished with gay chintz and women were taking off the stains of travel in its dressing room as they waited to say goodbye to their husbands, sons and sweethearts." With the enthusiastic support of the commanding officer, a program of service and hospitality was quickly under way. It was the first of a hundred and forty Hostess Houses, manned by volunteer hostesses who thronged to serve in them. They mushroomed over the country, in Army training camps, naval stations, marine and hospital camps, embarkation and debarkation ports.

YWCA experience with women workers in industry, Negro women and girls, the foreign-born, was put to work in the wartime situation. Service centers featuring good cafeterias, room registry and recreation were established in twenty industrial areas where women were pouring in to work in munitions and other plants. Especially for Negro women, Hostess Houses were built in seventeen camps and forty-nine communities, and service centers were opened in eight industrial areas. It was a period of intense nationalism in the United States. For foreign-born women and their families, the YWCA's International Translation and Service Bureau, family centers in immigrant communities near camps and munitions plants, special services for families of enlisted men and for location of refugees, were a boon. The National Board's health education program, directed by Dr. Anna Brown, arranged a series of lectures which reached over a million women and girls in 1,200 communities and inspired the War Department to institute a women's section in its Division of Social Hygiene.

War work overseas, our historian tells us, was not initiated by the National Board, but was undertaken in response to appeals from abroad, both from countries which had a YWCA and those which did not. The first request was from Russian women in Petrograd in the spring of 1917, but very shortly, the work was withdrawn as "the political conditions were changing rapidly," and no further work was done there until 1921 when Russian-speaking YWCA workers went in to assist with refugee work of the American Relief Association. In the summer of 1917 requests for help came from France and Poland. Eventually, a total of four hundred and seven workers went into nine countries, attired in the YWCA gray-blue uniform and wearing tricorn hats. Under the slogan "In Service for the Girls of the World," they established and ran clubs, hostess houses and service centers for girls and women on jobs attached to the military services, nurses, women munition workers, foreign war brides of American servicemen and refugees.

Many of the overseas workers had never been in a foreign country, but they quickly won their way—sometimes by sheer determination. One of the first who went to France was Mary Dingman, a seasoned YWCA worker who went on to work in the World's YWCA and eventually the United Nations. Miss Dingman was dubbed "Mademoiselle Il-le-Faut" by the French Army officers to whom she kept insisting that the girls *must* have centers, *must* have hot lunches, *must* have the opportunity to learn what the war was all about.

Every night for months Vera Cushman was on the train between visits to hostess houses and service centers. When she toured a hostess house, recalls a volunteer of those days, "you could see her looking alertly about. She saw immediately if anything was missing or not quite right, and took in everything from the reading material on the table to the garbage pails at the back door. She was always thinking up ideas about improvements for comfort or better service."

Both on the road and at headquarters she met with groups of volunteers. "She had them working like beavers," Emma Speer said. "She was a born organizer and very statesmanlike. I can see her now, getting one woman back on the track of discussion, curbing the uninformed enthusiasm of another, always holding them to the basic principles of the YWCA. She could talk anybody's language—volunteers, staff, army generals. And what a loose rein she used!"

It was not only with government officials and the military that Mrs. Cushman and her fellow council members were called upon to exercise "feminine statesmanship." Early in the days of the War Council, she was called on by upper-echelon officials of one of the men's agencies in the group designated by the government for war service. She invited Abby Aldrich Rockefeller, a prominent National Board member and chairman of an important committee of the War Work Council, to help receive them. Like Mrs. Cushman, Mrs. Rockefeller was noted for her beauty, charm and firm character. The meeting took place at YWCA headquarters.

"You never saw such exquisite creatures," recalls a staff member who was on hand that afternoon. "One wore a pink hat that looked like a piece of confection. The other wore an elegant large white hat. They came out of the meeting as they went in—relaxed, gracious, poised. The men were visibly downcast. Come to find out, the agency was proposing that the YWCA 'combine' with them for war work, which really meant they wanted to take over direction of YWCA workers, to say nothing of our war work budget!" With courtesy and firmness, the offer was refused.

It is understandable that men, accustomed to the "women's auxiliary" pattern of organization so common in churches and men's service agencies, found the YWCA somewhat puzzling. It was certainly no "auxiliary," yet it was not quite like such independent groups as those allied with the woman suffrage movement. It seems likely that the women of the YWCA in those days were too busy becoming what they would be to spend much time in self-analysis, and they themselves would not have been able to characterize the organization they were building. Vera Cushman, in a statement for the National Board in the first postwar years, went to the heart of that matter:

"We are the greatest and strongest group of women ever formed—I mean of women, by women and for women. We ought to be watchers of the skies, with the widest vision, the deepest sympathy, the most sensitive outreach, the longest look ahead and the most limitless courage. We ought to be inclusive, inspiring, prophetic."

During the war years, Vera Cushman's staff partner and the YWCA's representative at the inter-agency meetings of the seven organizations was the gentle and generous Helen Alling Davis, a Wellesley graduate who had been employed in YWCAs since graduation and now had experience in local, regional and national work. "I think my chief contribution," she told amused colleagues, "is to rise every few minutes in every meeting and say '*and women.*'" Three decades later Emma Speer said in speaking of Miss Davis, "If the organizations learned anything about women's place, needs and contributions—and somebody must have learned something, since the YWCA was pressed into service even before World War II began—it was due to her 'and women's!'"

After the Armistice in November, 1918, the War Work Council's programs at home were either discontinued or incorporated into established YWCAs. Some workers were demobilized, but many continued in YWCA work for the rest of their professional lives. Because of the great need for assistance in postwar Europe, YWCA overseas workers remained at full complement. At the request of governments or women's groups, some were assigned to help start new YWCAs and others to assist existing YWCAs rebuild program and leadership. When the War Work Council was dissolved in October, 1920, this substantial overseas work was transferred to the National Board's Foreign Division.

In the summer of 1919 Vera Cushman and five other American women went to Washington to receive the Distinguished Service Medal. Six months later she was invited to the Philadelphia Navy Yard to christen "The Blue Triangle," one of seven ships named in tribute to the organizations that had given service during the war. Only days before the event, Prohibition had gone into effect. Partly because of the temperance sentiment among YWCA members and partly to observe the letter of the law, she was bidden to request a bottle of spring water for the christening rather than the traditional champagne. The new ship's crew refused to man a ship not properly launched—it was bad luck! A compromise was reached, and on a frigid January morning Mrs. Cushman, "looking very much the grande dame," reports a witness, broke the bottle of spring water over the bow, while someone stationed at the stern, out of sight of the assembled crowd, carried out the time-honored tradition properly.

Vera Cushman was an "all-round" National Board member, interested in all aspects of YWCA work, but there is no doubt that in the postwar years she thought increasingly in global terms, and her primary interest was in international fields. She was a member, and for fifteen years a vice-president, of the World's Council, the legislative body of the World's YWCA. She helped organize the World Service Council, a venture of the YWCA of the U.S.A. to ensure continuing service to the YWCAs of other countries. She served on boards sponsoring church foreign missions and Christian education in China. As she had traveled through the United States in wartime, now she traveled the globe—to Europe, to South America, the Near East, China, India.

She made friends for her causes wherever she went — on steamships, in government circles, in business groups. Emma Speer, who sometimes traveled with her, told how quick she was to see "what life meant to the youngest stewardess on the ship as clearly as to the captain at whose table she sat." She was sharply aware, Mrs. Speer went on to say, that "the status of women was changing overnight in many countries, and that new patterns of life had to be made to ensure for girls places of self-respect, dignity and usefulness." This, they both believed, the YWCA was able to do.

She made a continuous effort to deepen her own understanding of people of other countries and to help others to do so. Those who saw her in action still remember how, "with utmost tact and warmth," she helped to draw together the French and German delegations at the first postwar meeting of the World's YWCA at Champéry, Switzerland, in 1920, and with what skill she helped to hostess its 1938 meeting in Muskoka, Canada, when nerves were tense because of the lowering shadows in Europe.

Vera Cushman died in Savannah, Georgia, on February 1, 1946. Her funeral, attended by four hundred people, was held at the First Presbyterian Church in New York City where she had been a member since she had come to the city as a bride. In a letter to *The New York Times,* Oswald Garrison Villard, the former editor of *The Nation,* wrote that she "was one of that all too small group of men and women who go far toward offsetting this city's crass materialism, who give it spiritual aims," and that she was "one of the city's greatest human assets, whose influence and radiance will continue to inspire others."

CHAPTER SEVEN

Martha Boyden Finley

The Whole World in Her Heart

Looking Backward to childhood, Martha Finley's daughter Ellen wrote of her mother, "She seemed to me like a round, comfortable, old-fashioned stove that sat right in the middle of the house and warmed every room! The one thing wrong with this image is the 'sitting'—as she was almost constantly in motion. She ran with little short steps, heels tapping vigorously on the floor—not high heels, sensible ones. She was a direct, honest, whole-hearted person who threw herself completely into whatever she did."

About five feet tall, a little plump, blue-eyed, Martha Finley had long brown hair which she wore coiled into a figure eight on top of her head, firmly secured with curved bone hairpins. Although she lived to the age of ninety, her hair never turned completely gray. She wore no makeup except a bit of powder, and didn't really need it, being one of those lucky persons with a natural fresh-complected look about her.

An early waker and riser, she came to full energy the minute she opened her eyes and hopped out of bed. With scarcely a look in the mirror, she twisted her hair in place, dressed for the day and never gave her appearance another thought. To her children, she seemed like a lark, she loved the morning so much, but when it came to breakfast, she was not at all bird-like. Oatmeal with cream, two eggs, bacon, toast and jam was her favorite menu.

A family woman to the core, she loved to cook and sew and when her children were small, made most of their clothes. Always impatient to get where she was going, she often crossed in the middle of a street, rarely waited for a green light. Her way of expressing herself was as direct as her locomotion, and her speech was salted with sayings handed down from her New England ancestors: "hot as tophet," "look like tunket," "independent as a hog on ice," "scarce as hen's teeth," "butter wouldn't melt in her mouth." Extremely generous in her contributions to deserving causes and in gifts to her family, she was economical when it came to things for herself. Unconcerned with changing styles, she bought clothes of good material and cut, and wore them as long as they held together. She couldn't abide materials she thought "sleazy."

All her life she had a deep feeling for family ties, and often her children teased her about her complete devotion to anyone who was related to her by blood, for it seemed literally nothing was too much to do for them.

Born Martha Boyden in the little town of Sheffield, Illinois, on July 21, 1866, she was one of a family of five and the only daughter. Her father had come to Sheffield from Massachusetts at the age of seventeen and opened a bank, and her mother's family, the Webbs, had come to Illinois from Maine shortly afterward. The Boydens were Congregationalists and Mr. Boyden was a deacon in the church.

When she was sixteen, Martha entered Knox College in Galesburg, Illinois, a campus that had become famous a quarter century before as the scene of the Lincoln-Douglas debates. In her class was eighteen-year-old John Finley, who had just finished a two-year teaching stint to earn the money for his tuition. It was love at first sight for the young man, but it was to be ten years before they married. By that time, he was well away on a distinguished career in higher education and had been appointed president of Knox. Martha had spent a year abroad after graduation, then a number of years quietly at home caring for her mother, who had become an invalid, and keeping house for her father.

Upon her marriage Mrs. Finley, whose husband was of Scotch-Irish descent with several Presbyterian ministers in his background, joined the Presbyterian Church. Obedience to the law of Christian love was the firm center of her being, and it was her joy to give herself wholeheartedly to prayer, daily Bible reading, and to the life of the church.

"Her children and grandchildren delighted in trying to stump her by asking the hardest questions in the old-fashioned Bible game," wrote her daughter, "but they were almost never successful. She rarely missed a Sunday at church. When asked if she were going to church, she replied promptly, 'It's Sunday, isn't it?'"

She gave herself the special mission of improving the lot of women everywhere, especially through opportunity for higher education. As time went on life brought to her the scope for her goals. When the Finleys moved East shortly after the turn of the century, she was appointed to the Board of Managers of the Women's Board of Foreign Missions of the Presbyterian Church; later, to its National Board of Foreign Missions. Her two favorite projects were the committee administering the Sage Fund (for the advance of women through schools, hospitals and missionary work) and the women's missionary magazine, *Outreach.*

Although, as a pastor friend of hers remarked, "her horizons were coterminous with the globe," the Near East and China held special appeal for her. She was a trustee of the Near East Foundation and for many years president of the Friends of the Near East. The College for Women at Yenching University in Peiping claimed her loyalty not only during its burgeoning days but doubly so in the dark days of World War II, during the hard, worrisome work of the return and rehabilitation of the many faculty members and students seized by the Japanese.

The Finleys lived for a time in Princeton, where Dr. Finley taught at the University, then in Albany during his years as New York State Commissioner of Education, and finally in New York City where he was president of the College of the City of New York before joining the editorial staff of *The New York Times.*

During the Princeton years, they became close friends of their neighbors, the Grover Clevelands. The former U.S. president, when he returned to private life in 1897, had gone back into law practice and was living quietly in Princeton and working on a book. Mrs. Finley, as adept at cribbage as she had once been on the tennis court, was his favorite adversary over the cribbage board. By a tragic coincidence, the same heartbreak struck the two households almost at the same time when each lost the eldest daughter in a diphtheria epidemic. Thereafter they were inseparable, and Mrs. Finley looked upon Frances Cleveland—later Frances Preston—as her closest friend. The two families bought adjoining properties in the little town of Tamworth, New Hampshire, where Mrs. Finley's great-grandfather Boyden had been the village doctor, and built summer homes within hailing distance of each other.

It was in this old New England setting, close to her ancestral roots, that Martha Finley was most comfortable. Every summer for fifty years, she kept open house for children, grandchildren, relatives and friends. She loved every moment of it, and took great pride in providing bountiful meals—fresh vegetables from her garden, homemade raspberry ice cream, apple pie and freshly-churned butter. She and Mrs. Preston had tea together every summer afternoon and celebrated their joint birthday at a big family picnic each July 21. Dr. Finley, too, was in his element, for he loved nature and the out of doors. To say he was a great walker is to understate the case; it is said that his idea of a Sunday stroll was to walk around Manhattan Island. Even today with many of Manhattan's landmarks gone, a plaque remains on the walk along the East River marking the "John Finley Walk," one of his favorites. At Tamworth he cut trails through the woods, built a chapel in a natural woodsy spot, and wrote many poems about the area, always with the flavor of the classic past which was very real to him.

The son of her beloved neighbors once wrote of Mrs. Finley and his boyhood summer recollections for the county newspaper in New Hampshire. Hearing her brisk footsteps on the porch next door, he said, "was a sure sign summer had begun, and a satisfying, comfortable promise that all was right with the world." Remarking that she had never learned to drive a car, he recalled the summer day when she had upset the democrat—a kind of horse-drawn station wagon—in the driveway, to the consternation of everyone but herself. It was the measure of the woman that she "had gone from the day of the carriage and oxen to the day of the auto, bulldozer and airplane, assimilating the changes with notable good humor and interest."

One could not put this rare woman in a category, he wrote. "Her life was compounded of poetry and practicality. Her interests were vast but she had the rare quality of being concerned also with the little pleasantly gossippy things of life. Her curiosity, though sometimes sharply phrased, sprang from a deep and serious anxiety to set things right. Planning for others was one of her delights and no one she loved has ever entirely escaped her affectionately-conceived time tables!"

The lad now grown to manhood in a rapidly-changing world and remembering his mother's good friend summed up the quality which made such a memorable impression upon him. "She had an oddly tolerant type of spiritual rigidity with tender solicitude and unfailing interest in everyone she knew. Despite her high moral standards, she never shrugged people off but patiently and warmly evaluated them. She never wanted to stand idly by, but wanted to be in the fray from the outset. Her deep and simple religious faith made it impossible for her to think ill of anyone, yet whatever there was, she wanted to know the truth of it and if possible to straighten it out."

Mrs. Finley was in her early fifties when she and her husband came to New York City to live and joined the First Presbyterian Church. Mary French and Vera Cushman were members of the congregation. These women who had so many interests and concerns in common gravitated toward each other. Mrs. Finley had become interested in the YWCA during her years in Albany. Now she was elected to the National Board and almost at once was appointed chairman of the Foreign Division (later the International Division). Very soon she became a vice-president and member of the Executive Committee of the National Board.

The YWCA's postwar work in Europe and China was at its height. The farflung operations of the War Work Council had been turned over to the Foreign Division to administer, and several hundred YWCA workers were abroad running hostess houses and canteens, working with migrants, refugees, war brides, war babies, orphans, munitions workers. Even in disrupted Europe they were trying, as they were in China, to train indigenous leadership and to encourage women to learn better health care for their families and to advance themselves through education and training for employment.

Joyfully, Martha Finley plunged into the work. It was as though all she had been and done and cared about had prepared her for these years of overflowing opportunity. Her brisk little heels tapped in and out of offices on the twelfth floor where the Foreign Division's headquarters offices were housed, in and out of committee meeting rooms, in and out of administrative offices. Trains carried her the length and breadth of the United States as, with other board members, she stumped the country in behalf of the World Service Council. A charter member of the council, she served for some years as its vice president. Generous in her own contributions, she continued frugal in her personal expenditures. Her traveling companions chuckle to remember how she rode in the coaches by day, going into the Pullman cars only for the sleeping hours.

Under her chairmanship the work overseas extended into Turkey, Latvia, Estonia. An indefatigable voyager, she made many trips to Europe and the Near East, combining admirably her job as American representative on the World's YWCA Council and her responsibility for the overseas work of both the National Board and the Presbyterian Mission Board. Wherever she went, she kept an eye out for opportunities to put into practice her personal gospel on the advancement of women. Her successor as chairman of the Foreign Division Committee, Mrs. Maurice T. Moore, once told of Mrs. Finley's influence on the American Farm School near Salonika, where the Finleys had often visited, for Greece was a land beloved of them both. Originally the school had been set up to train men in modern farm methods, and Mrs. Finley had tried to persuade them to open their courses to women, too. After some years of experience the school officials had changed their policy, finding her reasoning completely sound; their earliest men graduates had abandoned what they had been taught because the village women did not understand the reasons for the change from ancient custom.

To Mrs. Finley each YWCA worker in the foreign field was a special friend, almost a member of the family. When they came home on furlough, she insisted she be allowed to entertain them in her home *first,* before they began their round of social and speaking engagements, and took great pleasure in serving them hearty American meals—a roast, potatoes, green vegetables, a good dessert.

Her home at the foot of Lexington Avenue, overlooking Gramercy Park, and the summer house in Tamworth were often the background for personal chats and small group meetings, when she encouraged the returnees to talk about their experiences and if they wished, about their personal lives and problems. It was her tradition to give a breakfast, an elaborate and special affair, for foreign staff members who were home on furlough at convention time. It was said that some went out of their way to make sure to go to convention so as not to miss the event!

From these breakfast reunions grew that flourishing organization, the "XFs," to which former foreign staff belong. At Christmas she sent each person connected with the Foreign Division a red and blue calendar—always the same kind each year—with a word of personal greeting. Those in New York City, no less than those in far-off places, looked forward to finding "Mrs. Finley's calendar" in their Christmas mail.

Board and committee meetings were enlivened by her presence. Although conservatively inclined in some ways, if her feelings were touched she spoke without fear or reservation while more cautious folk pondered the ifs, ands and buts. Emma Speer wrote of her that "when talk seemed to take the place of action, she was 'an unhesitating discourager of hesitancy,' and her wisdom and fearlessness endeared her to the presiding officer!"

As the postwar days went on, isolationism began to gain a foothold in the United States and an international point of view such as Mrs. Finley's was not very popular with those members of the National Board who reflected this trend. Serene in her convictions, she missed no opportunity to advance the cause of the National Board's foreign work and to point up the significance of the World's YWCA, and in the end she carried most of the board along with her. In budget discussions she watched like a hawk to make sure the Foreign Division got its share; if there was danger that it wouldn't, she would jump to her feet and vigorously remonstrate with her fellow board members.

To argue with her under such circumstances would be to threaten the goose that laid the golden egg: of all the gifted money-raisers the National Board has seen in its sixty years, she still holds one of the top places. "She was a marvel at it," her daughter wrote. "One of the reasons was that she wrote persuasive letters and then the minute the check came she wrote and mailed a gracious thank-you letter. She was an impulsive person and liked to do things the minute she thought of them. She wrote eight or ten letters a day and saw to it that they were mailed immediately."

She was just as persuasive with the spoken word. Once she called on a Japanese restaurant owner in New York City to ask for a contribution to a scholarship fund to enable Japanese girls to come to the United States for YWCA training. The staff member who accompanied her wondered whether or not Mrs. Finley's enthusiastic talk about "these fine Christian girls" was leaping the language barrier, but concluded that something got through to him when he agreed to give a substantial sum. The next day a perspiring restaurateur visited the headquarters office to find out just what he had agreed to!

One can only conclude that Mrs. Finley's secret lay in her mastery of the art of communication. She had such good relationships with those she wrote annually for contributions to the National Board that when she reached the forgetful age and wrote letters she forgot to sign, her contributors recognized her writing and sent their checks as usual.

Many honors came to her in her lifetime. Knox College bestowed upon her an honorary degree for her work in "international relations, Christian missions and social welfare." She was cited by the Presbyterian Church for fifty years' continuous service to her two favorite projects, the Sage Fund and *Outreach*, the women's missionary magazine. In behalf of the National Board, she received the Order of the Red Cross of Estonia for the work in developing a YWCA there. The Martha Finley Scholarships were set up by the Foreign Division for the training of leaders in YWCAs of other countries.

Mrs. Finley lived to see the YWCA's one hundredth birthday in this country. In 1955, at the age of eighty-nine, she served as co-chairman of the Centennial Fund Committee. She died at her daughter's home in Atlanta, Georgia, in the fall of 1956, three months after her ninetieth birthday. At a memorial service at the National Board the following February, Sarah Lyon, executive of the Foreign Division during the burgeoning 1920s—and the hard-pressed 1930s—talked of her "faith which dispelled the shadows of the earth."

"The hardest experience of her life," said Miss Lyon, "came during the Depression days when so much of our work had to be curtailed. But she worked harder, never seemed to be depressed, and over and over again at a meeting where we faced some insuperable task, it would suddenly become superable because of her courage, determination and faith."

More recently another staff member who knew Martha Finley well summed up in a few words the essence of the woman and the legacy she left to all of us: "She was loved because she *was* what she believed."

CHAPTER EIGHT

Florence Simms

Symbol of Social Conscience

"I FEEL very much at home today. You sent us out fifteen years ago in this industrial department to find out things for you . . . we have come back to tell you what we have found. . . . It is a family gathering, quite a section of humanity here this morning. The message of Christ, if it is practically applied, will save our industrial situation in America and in the world. I believe that if we accept this thing on legislation . . . it will make us stand with forward-looking employers whose only hope [against] unjust and unfair competition is through legislation [and will] help us stand with the labor people who want a proper and constructive way of finding themselves and expressing themselves without revolution. I believe it is the only effective way of helping to do the thing . . . we believe in. Why, my friends, we could not bring a thing less than this and bring anything at all."

Thus Florence Simms, national industrial secretary of the National Board, reached the culmination of seventeen years' hard work in establishing the YWCA's industrial program as an integral part of a Christian organization of Christian social principles. The tall, auburn-haired woman, addressing the Sixth National Convention of the YWCA of the U.S.A. on an April day in 1920, now had less than three years more to live, but in these moments she was putting the finishing touches on an extraordinary contribution to the organization that had claimed her loyalty for nearly thirty years.

Daisy Florence Simms—she was "Daisy" until she graduated from college and entered her first job—was born April 17, 1873, in Rushville, Indiana. Her father, Michael Simms, the fourth generation of a Virginia family of English extraction, had wandered to Kentucky and on to the Midwest. Her mother, Jane Amanda Taylor Simms, had been born and brought up in Homer, Indiana.

A YWCA staff member who knew Miss Simms' parents says, "Her father was a pioneer, a homespun philosopher type. He was a not very successful farmer, but an entertaining and very bright man. Her mother was an earnest Methodist. I always thought Florence got her father's brains and her mother's religion." Daisy Florence and Eva, a younger sister, were the only two children. Eva, a frail girl, died in 1910 after she had been married only a short time.

As a school girl, Daisy did well scholastically but was better known as an elocutionist. When she was sixteen, she was a finalist in the Demorest contests, an institution founded by a wealthy New York man to offer prizes for the best renditions of compositions on temperance. An Indiana newspaper, reporting on her excellent performance, added that "her form is slender, her face spirituelle, her eyes glorious orbs, full of expression." Daisy took second place that year, but the next, 1890, she won the gold medal with a recitation called "Young America's War Cry." The following year she was one of four graduates of the Rushville High School. Her commencement oration, "Forward," reflects, says her biographer, "her early religious conservatism [but shows that she] would develop a liberal outlook upon the whole of life."

She won a scholarship to De Pauw University, where she graduated from the College of Liberal Arts in 1895 with the degree of Bachelor of Philosophy. In history, political science and English literature, she did particularly well. The president of the university, J. P. D. John, wrote of her in a letter recommending her for a teaching position, that she was "a young woman of marked ability, dignity and pleasant disposition" and that she "stands high in the estimation of both faculty and students." Her class chose her to deliver an oration and to present their gift to the university.

As a college student, her two main interests were temperance —Frances Willard was her heroine—and women's rights. College friends remarked on "the bright and humorous way in which she pleaded the cause of women." To the YWCA student Association and other religious activities on the campus, she gave considerable time and energy. She was a member of Kappa Alpha Theta sorority, but was independent about allowing this small circle to restrict her campus friendships. Her independence also extended in other directions; she scorned the "clinging vine" role which was assumed by many women students to be the essence of a woman's relationships with men, regardless of how it suited a particular female's personality.

Although she had intended to teach, she was appointed immediately after graduation to the student staff at the Chicago headquarters of the American Committee of the YWCA. After a summer of training she began the job in September, 1895. For two years she traveled in states of the upper Mississippi Valley, organizing and stimulating student Associations on campuses of girls' schools and women's colleges. In this work she was associated with Clarissa Spencer, who was later to become the second general secretary of the World's YWCA. "We were both very young and immature in many ways, very earnest and zealous," Miss Spencer recalled in a note to Miss Simms' biographer, "and both ready to get all the fun out of every situation that we could!" She was impressed, Miss Spencer said, "by Florence's good looks and her fine bearing, her strong convictions," and how simple and sincere she was. Once at a conference they met "a cocksure

Christian worker" who criticized one of the other conferees for her "lack of spiritual grace." Looking back and comparing them, Miss Spencer said, "That summer I realized that Miss Simms, with her simple, honest, humble spirit, was the better Christian."

From 1897 to 1904, Florence Simms worked as a YWCA executive, first in the city Associations of Portland, Maine, and Binghamton, New York, and finally on the Michigan State Committee. While she was on this last job, her interest in women industrial workers came to the fore at a time when this was a growing interest of the American Committee. In 1904 she and Helen Barnes were appointed secretaries at the committee's Chicago headquarters, with responsibility for the industrial work. Three years later they went to New York to continue this assignment for the new National Board, with Miss Simms becoming the head of the industrial department.

"She was nearly six feet tall, big-boned, and had that excellent posture that makes for a handsome physique," a staff member describes her. "She had red-brown hair, pale gray eyes that could get quite a spark in them, and a beautiful complexion and high coloring." She was more of an "idea person" than an administrator and always had people around her to whom she could assign the more detailed part of the work.

"She was a deep-feeling person, often impatient. When she got angry she used the staff as a safety valve, so that in public or at meetings she could express herself heatedly but was always under control. One of her greatest values to the National Board—and to the work she did so well—was that her convictions were so deep that she made herself felt even with those who utterly disagreed with her."

Her upbringing in the pioneer climate of the Midwest ingrained in her a sense of respect for the individual, an essential for a career such as hers. Because of it, however, she found herself at odds with some people she met in New York. "In those days," explains a staff member who worked closely with her, "the prevailing respect in the East was for money and prestige. There was a definite sense of class structure and even very good people accepted as fact that 'lower classes' were inferior to them. Often when people expressed themselves in this way, she would say, 'Yes, but they are *people,* aren't they?' "

She had followed the doctrines instilled in her by her mother and was inclined to take a somewhat narrow view of religion. In New York she was exposed to scholars and thinkers who were "interpreting the Bible from the point of view of history," as a YWCA Training School graduate puts it, and the "social gospel" writings of Walter Rauschenbusch of the Rochester Theological Seminary. Not without pain she began to evolve a philosophy which, in the words of a close friend, "integrated within her the social respect for the individual and her own true religious convictions to form the basis for her work and personal life."

It took a while for YWCA secretaries to recognize that the uppermost needs of young women workers in industry—in the YWCA jargon of the day, they were known as "industrial girls"—were not spiritual needs. Florence Simms once described in a speech her earliest work in the light of later insight: "We had meetings at noon in the factories at which we presented our kind of religion. The girls were wonderful. They really listened. I am ashamed to tell you now I do not know what wages they earned or what hours they worked. I was struggling for a religious life and supposed they were, too. I went on for several years, trying to make them see what I saw, think what I thought, get what I wanted them to have, which was primarily religion."

Like social workers today whose job is to help hard-to-reach groups, the secretaries tried first one thing, then another, to find out what they could do to help that would be acceptable to the girls. The first breakthrough came when the secretaries caught hold of the idea that "the only way to develop girls is to give them a chance to develop themselves." Self-governing clubs were organized, and the secretaries began to move into the role of advisor or consultant and to encourage leadership to emerge from the group itself. As the girls planned their own programs it became clear that the bread-and-butter matters of living, better jobs and more education were their real concerns. By 1915, there were 375 such clubs sponsored by YWCAs. Clubs in the same cities or areas formed federations; the federations in a region met together, beginning in 1913. Regional and national summer conferences were held, and eventually, in 1922, a representative national group was formed, the Industrial Assembly.

Secretaries and board members who worked on this "extension program"—so designated because they went into the factories with the program rather than conducting it in the central buildings—learned to make a practical approach. A local board member from Pennsylvania, telling about going into factories in her city beginning in 1910, says, "When we found the girls were illiterate, we first told stories from the Bible and the classics, then when they got interested, we helped them learn to read. Gradually we learned about their working conditions: no place to eat lunch, no place to wash, only two toilets for three hundred girls. Some of the girls got lead poisoning from eating lunch at their work benches, a fact we confirmed by taking them to our own doctors. We went to the employer. He raised Cain but had to do something about it.

"We could see the problem couldn't be licked by taking on employers one by one, however. It called for state legislation. We went to the state Capitol to testify for a woman's labor law, which was finally passed in 1913. One of the provisions was for an eight-hour day, something the men had already won through collective bargaining. Today it is hard to believe that employers were incensed at women's trying to get it, too. On the same train with us were some three hundred men representing the industries. When they realized we two women were going to oppose them, they were furious. It just so happened that we both held large blocks of stock in some of their companies. Otherwise they would probably have just laughed at us."

In 1906 the executive committee of the World's YWCA decided that a major topic of discussion at its world meeting in Berlin in 1910 should be the place of the YWCA in social and industrial life. Florence Simms was asked to chair an international commission to study the subject. The commission report, which she presented at the Berlin meeting and to which she always referred as "the charter" of YWCA industrial work, recognized "the social significance of the teachings of Jesus," and urged all national Associations to study the social problems of the day, especially as they affected the lives of young women.

The following year, at the biennial convention of the YWCA in Indianapolis, resolutions based on the commission's report were adopted. The National Board's report, "Fifty Years of Social Action," published in 1963, credits this formal action committing the YWCA to "educating the public on the need for a living wage for women and the need to support legislation which would regulate hours and wages of working women," as the beginning of social action in the organization.

Florence Simms' knowledge of social conditions and the lives of women workers in countries all over the world was invaluable in the YWCA's World War I work with war-production workers both at home and overseas. At war's end, the number of YWCA industrial clubs had increased from 375 to 823, the number of secretaries on local industrial jobs had risen from 97 to 365, and her own headquarters staff numbered thirty.

As her experience and knowledge grew, so her convictions deepened. She felt it was not enough that the YWCA should sponsor the industrial program—the times demanded that a Christian organization should take a stand for Christian social principles. In her work with other national movements such as the Women's Trade Union League, the Consumer's League and the Federal Council of Churches, she discussed these thoughts. She became very interested in a statement adopted by the Council of Churches in 1912. Titled the "Social Ideals of the Churches," it constituted a social platform of sixteen items, calling for equal rights and justice "for all men in all stations of life," abolition of child labor, regulation of working conditions for women, "the right of employees and employers alike to organize and for adequate means of conciliation and arbitration in industrial disputes," and reforms on wages and working hours. Other items anticipated some of today's accepted facts of working life, such as workman's compensation, unemployment insurance, and old age and survivors insurance.

Miss Simms proposed to the National Board in 1918 that it recommend to the 1920 convention, to be held in Cleveland, adoption of the "Social Ideals" as the YWCA's social platform. Her proposal touched off two years of heated debate; the reaction ranged from enthusiasm to horror.

"Many of our board women were shocked at the inhuman aspects of what was going on in industry," says a former staff member. "When they learned more about it, they felt guilty about their own privileges and determined to take some action. It has never been fully appreciated what a struggle some of them went through and with what integrity they acquitted themselves. The stand they took was, in some cases, a threat to their marriages and family life, but they stood firm because they were convinced it was right."

Others were more shocked at the "Social Ideals" than they were at the working conditions of their industrial members, either because of their own point of view or the influence of their husbands. When Florence Simms dined in homes of board members, she was often challenged by the husbands. One evening she and two of her staff members were bidden to the home of a board member who had inherited a considerable fortune and was married to a railroad executive. One of the staff members tells the story: "We were not well-fed to begin with. I remember we were served roast pork which was underdone. All evening our host harangued us about our 'socialistic beliefs.' Miss Simms was pretty good at such discussions, but finally lost her temper. 'Well, Mr. ——,' she said, 'if we do have a revolution, it will be people like you that bring it on.' So saying, she put on her hat and majestically led us from the house. He stalked from the room, and we could hear him pounding away on the huge pipe organ in their music room as we walked down the street."

In the end, the "Social Ideals" became one of six recommendations from the National Board to the convention in 1920 concerning study of social conditions, social action and the principles upon which these would be based. On the convention's fourth day, April 16, with Theresa Wilbur Paist presiding, the recommendations were introduced.

"We believe," read the preamble, "that in Jesus Christ is to be found the solution of the world's need. In every age some great issue stands out as a challenge to Christianity. Today this challenge is found in our economic life and social relationships. The way in which Christian people and Christian organizations meet such issues furnishes a searching test of the reality of Christian experience."

As it had in the National Board discussions, debate centered on the recommendations "to adopt the 'Social Ideals of the Churches' as the YWCA social platform" and "to make a careful study of the social and economic conditions affecting women, and the possibilities of improvement through legislation; and to use [YWCA] resources and influence to help secure such legislation as will promote the welfare of young women."

Several city Association delegates spoke in favor, in somewhat the same vein as one from Freeport, Illinois: "Do we as Christian women really want other women to work nights and seven days a week [so] that we may have more leisure and more things?" Others spoke from experience in social action, as did a delegate from Tacoma, Washington: "We have written to our senators and representatives by the hundreds . . . have voted intelligently and have ameliorated the conditions of women to a marked degree. We are having a power put in our hands that we must use. Do not be afraid of it."

Women workers, Association members, also spoke, a worker from a Pennsylvania silk mill pleading, "I beg of you to be the leaven among the girls in industry and help them rise to better conditions . . . and to give them a more abundant life." Student delegates and industrial committee members added their sentiments in favor. During the discussion, some speakers referred delicately to "the present unrest," and one suggested that perhaps the word "agreement" might be substituted for "bargaining." Another delegate took a no-nonsense attitude to the suggestion, saying the term "collective bargaining" was "so well known around the world that in some languages it is one word," and that to change it would create confusion as to the meaning.

From the opposition came the opinion of one delegate that it was "all right to study these things," but she thought the part about helping secure legislation should be dropped. A National Board member who had fought against the report from the beginning told the convention she had sought advice from "one of our great economists," and she read the wire she had received from him that day: "Taking part as Associations in current politics is most unwise, however praiseworthy for members as individuals." She was alarmed by "the trend of our time toward radical socialism, a trend which I regret to say I have found even in certain departments of our Association that we love so much."

As the session drew to a close, Florence Simms rose and began her remarks: "I feel very much at home today." Speaking slowly, easily, with obvious conviction, she talked about Christian social principles, what the women of the YWCA would be doing to help the present situation by working on legislation, and lastly what it meant to her to have "come home." "I think now it is no more the industrial department which is struggling [with these problems], but it is the whole of the organization."

After two days' debate, all six recommendations were accepted unanimously by the Convention.

In 1912 Florence Simms had suffered a breakdown from excessive fatigue following a long period of overwork. She was persuaded to take a vacation which she spent in Italy and from which she returned feeling restored to health. However, for the rest of her life she struggled against physical ailments and those who were closest to her believed she had never completely recovered. She died on January 6, 1923, in Mattoon, Illinois, where her parents then lived, a few days after a mastoid operation.

Less than seven years remained before a chain of events—the 1929 stock market crash, the economic depression, the rise of a strong labor movement, the passage of the Social Security Act—would introduce a new era in the United States. Though Florence Simms did not live to see these changes, so many of which she had foreseen, the work she had done and inspired others to do had made it possible for the YWCA to take its place in that new era.

CHAPTER NINE

Theresa Wilbur Paist

A Woman for All Seasons

IT'S AN APRIL DAY in 1964 in Cleveland, Ohio. The great hotel ballroom is jammed with more than twenty-four hundred voting and visiting delegates to the YWCA's 23rd National Convention, representing 368 community and student Associations from coast to coast and border to border. Enthusiastic applause follows the First Lady, Mrs. Lyndon B. Johnson, as she leaves the podium after addressing the delegates, escorted by the convention's presiding officer, Elizabeth Marvel. Members of the official party file from the ballroom. The television cameras are wheeled away. A buzz of interim conversation begins.

Now Mrs. Marvel returns, preceded by a tall, slim, brown-haired woman, whose erect carriage and brisk walk belie her eighty-plus years. The words of introduction are drowned out, for suddenly every person in the room is on her feet, applauding and cheering, while the speaker-to-be leans cozily on the podium, eyes twinkling, a half-smile playing over her face.

"Well now girls," says Theresa Paist, as the room quiets, glancing offstage to make sure the visitors are out of earshot, "you'll just have to come down to home fare."

The witty, warm and wise woman who presided over the YWCA's Sixth National Convention in this very city forty-four years ago—and the Seventh, Eighth and Ninth Conventions as well—is back at the podium. Those who remember the YWCA's history-making days of the 1920s are meeting a cherished old friend. Younger folk, with shorter memories, are face-to-face with a particularly folksy, approachable YWCA legend.

For over sixty years, Theresa Wilbur Paist has been a YWCA "woman for all seasons." She served on the staff in the pioneer days of the American Committee and was on the original staff of the National Board for its first five years. After her marriage and retirement from professional life and while bringing up three children, she worked as a volunteer on innumerable committees and commissions of the National Board; and with her left hand, so to speak, she did the work of president of a local Association. As president of the YWCA of the U.S.A., she presided over four conventions in the 1920s, including two of the most stormy and significant in YWCA annals. In the depression days of the 1930s she was president of the National Board for seven years. Today, an honorary member of the National Board and beloved "elder statesman," she lives tranquilly in California, always her home state no matter where she actually resided. Ever ready to write an article, give a speech, or fly off to represent the YWCA at a meeting, she seems to have an agreement with herself and the YWCA that "Wherever I'm needed, that's where I'll be."

Theresa Paist's parents, Dwight Locke Wilbur and Edna Marie Lyman Wilbur, were born in Ohio to families who had come from England by way of New England. Her father, a graduate of Western Reserve Seminary in Farmington, Ohio, served in the Civil War, then studied law at University of Michigan. Between them, he and his wife bequeathed both Quaker and Congregational traditions to their family. They had met in an Ohio town where he was the school teacher and she the daughter of a Congregational church deacon. It was a Wilbur family joke that the Lyman children were a trial to the schoolmaster because family prayers often made them late for school!

Always interested in newly-developing areas, Mr. and Mrs. Wilbur moved west by degrees — first to Boonesboro [now Boone], Iowa, where their six children were born, then to Jamestown, North Dakota, where Mr. Wilbur was land agent for the Northern Pacific Railroad, and finally, in 1887, to Riverside, California.

Theresa was the youngest of a lively and talented family. Her brothers, Curtis and Ray Lyman, held Cabinet positions in the Calvin Coolidge and Herbert Hoover administrations, respectively; and Ray Lyman Wilbur was president of Stanford University for nearly thirty years. Her sister Louise was a Presbyterian missionary in Persia, and another sister, Bertha, was a musician.

When the family settled in Riverside, Theresa was seven. The town itself was only nineteen years old, and the Wilburs enjoyed being pioneer residents. Mr. Wilbur was elected to the school board and became president of the Board of Trade.

"My father was very keen on developments in science and education, and in free thought of all kinds," Mrs. Paist said in a recent interview. "He was careful to do nothing to upset our religious zeal, but he wasn't too keen on such things as the whale swallowing Jonah. Once when an old-time evangelist was in town, my father remarked, 'I hear you have to be saved just his way.' Another time I heard him say, apropos of the supposed conflict between science and religion, that he always somehow felt science had not been much of a surprise to God!"

Mr. Wilbur was very enthusiastic about "Leland Stanford and his new university," and all the Wilbur children who came of university age after 1891 when it was opened to students were educated there. Theresa, who graduated in 1903, was president of the student YWCA and became friends with Harriet Taylor and Bertha Condé, who visited the campus as representatives of the American Committee.

After a year of teaching school in Pasadena, Theresa Wilbur

was appointed state secretary for the American Committee in California and Arizona. In Buffalo ("the farthest east I'd ever been") for the committee's national convention, she learned of the proposed merger with the International Board. Shortly afterward, she was brought to the committee's Chicago headquarters as a student secretary. She studied the comprehensive reports coming from the Joint Committee headed by Grace Dodge and, in due course, made two trips to New York City—one with staff members to meet Miss Dodge, and the second to be present at the convention in Old South Church in December, 1906, for "the great moment when the actual organization of the National Board took place."

Theresa Wilbur was one of twelve American Committee secretaries who moved to New York early in 1907 as staff members of the new National Board. She recalls that the roster included Harriet Taylor and Mabel Cratty, who headed the American Committee staff; Emma Hayes and two others who developed work in cities; Elizabeth Wilson, head of training; Florence Simms and Helen Barnes, industrial secretaries; Bertha Condé and Ruth Paxson, who shared student work with Miss Wilbur, and Frances Field, a former state secretary in the East who had acted as staff secretary to the Joint Committee. They were joined by Dr. Anna Brown, formerly employed as health education consultant by the International Board, who was, says Mrs. Paist, "at once loved and appreciated by all of us."

The professional workers were a puzzle to women formerly of the International Board. "Who really has the decisive power —the secretaries or the board women?" they would ask. "They didn't know what to make of us," chuckles Mrs. Paist, "and of course we hardly knew what to make of ourselves. They knew rich people, poor people and school teachers, but what was the status, if any, of YWCA secretaries!"

From a perspective of sixty years, she looks back on herself as a young worker in the new regime: "We probably seemed over eager to the New York women. I remember feeling we from Chicago were more modern and progressive, and that the work of the older city Associations was too static. After one meeting of students with older women in a city Association, one of the women expressed great satisfaction about younger people coming along to keep the work going. I thought privately if we couldn't do better than just to keep this type of work going, it was just too bad! But I felt much less cocky in later years when I myself was president of a big city Association."

If the professional staff was a new experience to the board, the reverse was also true. "We had to get used to their folkways, and what a struggle it was to guess what was expected of us in the opulent homes to which we were invited! We learned that at luncheons, hats were not removed. It was a good custom, because with the corsets we wore in those days, reaching our hands up to our heads was not easy! The first time a group of us were invited to dinner at Miss Dodge's home, we arrived and seeing no hats in the cloakroom, wondered 'Do they wear them at dinner, too?' Later we found nobody wore hats going to, at, or coming from, a dinner!"

Breakfast in bed was something Theresa Wilbur had previously been led to expect only when she was ill, but it proved to be the custom in many homes for both hostess and guest. Another strange "folkway" was having the maid unpack for overnight guests. Once at Greystone, Grace Dodge's home, Miss Wilbur forgot the slip for a light-colored dinner dress and hastily substituted her nightgown which was very similar. "I don't know what the maid thought when she unpacked for the other girls and put their nightgowns out on their beds but found none for me, it being on my person!"

A handy tip from a colleague who knew "the New York crowd" is still remembered by Mrs. Paist: "She carefully briefed me on the fact that families were so interrelated that I better make only good remarks about anyone to anyone!"

To combat the freezing New York winters, the transplanted Californian bought big furlined gloves ("Someone told me only streetcar conductors wore such gloves in New York") and had a muff and neckpiece made from leftover pieces of fur. "I called it Lazarus because it was made of bits from the rich man's table, that is, mink."

Theresa Wilbur's job took her to campuses over the country. In the fall of 1910, Mabel Cratty asked her to come to St. Louis after visits in that area, for a personal conversation. Miss Cratty proposed that Miss Wilbur transfer from the student department to take charge of organizing a "territorial committee" to extend YWCA work in Pennsylvania, Delaware and Maryland. It seemed an overwhelming change, but after some hesitation, she accepted the assignment.

Looking forward with something less than great confidence to January when the new job would begin, and disappointed at being too far away to go home to California for Christmas, Theresa Wilbur gladly fell in with a plan suggested by a fellow staff member, Louise Brooks, to spend the holidays that year at the Northfield Hotel in Massachusetts, the site of many summer student conferences.

At the hotel a group of young people, the Friendship Club, had gotten a gay winter sports program under way. The two girls were delighted to find among them some of their summer conference friends. Soon they had met everyone in the club, including Frederic Paist, a Philadelphia businessman. "When Fred found I was a Californian, he told me he had heard so much about Santa Barbara he planned to go there for his honeymoon. So I figured here was another fine young man who was already engaged—but he wasn't! Someone told him I was a sort of female YMCA secretary, but he seemed much more interested in the fact that my new job would bring me to Philadelphia now and then. . . . That winter and spring, the College Club there was our place to meet."

Both courtship and career were interrupted the next April when word came of Theresa's mother's serious illness. She left from Indianapolis, where she was attending the YWCA convention. Though she did not know it then, it was her last professional assignment. That summer, Mr. Paist went to California to see her and they became engaged. She remained there until her mother's death in December. In January, 1912, the Paists were married in California and went to Santa Barbara for their honeymoon. Their first home was in Langhorne, Pennsylvania, near Philadelphia, and, says Mrs. Paist, "I went right on helping with the territorial committee—only as a volunteer instead of a staff member."

If Theresa Paist's marriage brought an end to one career, it certainly marked the beginning of another; from then on she had a volunteer finger in nearly every important YWCA pie. Mr. Paist sometimes traveled with her on YWCA junkets and so did their children. Their elder daughter, Gertrude, was nicknamed the "world baby" by conferees at the World Student Christian Federation meeting at Lake Mohonk, New York, in the spring of 1913. Mrs. Paist, Gertrude and a nurse were placed in a room near enough the meeting room "so I could hear her if she cried from hunger," says Mrs. Paist, explaining that she breast-fed all her children and that "in those days you were supposed to nurse them for a year."

The same spring she decided against going to the YWCA convention in Richmond, Virginia, chiefly because the Philadelphia YWCA, in whose affairs she was deeply involved, was in the midst of a building fund campaign. In her absence, the convention appointed her chairman of an important national committee charged with making a study. During the two years of the study, her younger daughter, Frances, was born.

Historically speaking, the subject of the study is interesting. The student Associations that earlier had been insistent that the basis of YWCA membership be membership in a Protestant evangelical church were now asking the national Association to allow them to accept members on the basis of their personal beliefs, regardless of church affiliation. The issue of "church basis" versus "personal basis" was fated to be debated among YWCA members for seven years to come.

"The study committee was due to report to the 1915 convention in Los Angeles," writes Mrs. Paist. "Since my brother Curtis and sister Bertha had homes there, and various YWCA secretaries making the train trip vowed they would help take charge of the baby en route, I decided to go. At the last minute, my husband decided to come along. Baby Frances was six months old and nursing, and Gertrude was two and a half. All survived and had a good time, though Fred did not find the national secretaries expert at Rook (a kind of Presbyterian bridge) with which they helped to entertain him. I gave my report and the convention accepted it, but two conventions had to vote it before it could be part of the Constitution. The war intervened, so it was 1920 in Cleveland before the final vote could be taken."

The War Work Council, created by the National Board in 1917 to render wartime services, "was something new and different for all of us," says Mrs. Paist. "In those days, women weren't mixed up in such things. I was particularly interested in the plight of foreign-born families and the girls coming from country towns into war-production factories. Like everything else the YWCA has gone into, this wartime work started with the needs of our own members—women workers, girls of foreign-born families. We came out of the war with a very good reputation, I must say, and furthermore we had the pick of the crop for volunteers and staff."

The early postwar high spots, to Theresa Paist, were the 1920 convention in Cleveland, "where we made decisions that really shaped the future of the YWCA," and the establishment of the YWCA Retirement Fund, which she looks back on as "a good sound job of pioneering."

For the six years it took to make the Fund a going concern—it went into operation September 1, 1925—Mrs. Paist was a determined supporter of the not widely popular idea. "Security was not as fashionable as it is now," she points out, "and there was less warmth toward the idea of deductions from paychecks and contributions from employers."

She and others charged with proposing a suitable plan for YWCA secretaries found few existing pension plans to guide them. Nevertheless, they set themselves to master the complexities of such matters as liability and mortality tables and "credit for prior service." During one convention discussion of the proposed plan, suggestions more in line with customs of the day were made—Why not establish a home for retired workers? Why not set up a loan fund for needy older secretaries? After a bit, she told the convention, "We might as well realize that if we get into this, we get into it all over and we get into it together."

Her name was first on the list of those comprising the "body corporate" created by the Act of Incorporation of the Fund, passed by the New York State Legislature, and for twenty years she served as a Fund trustee.

In its 40th annual report, in which the Fund showed assets of $29 million, over two thousand participating staff members and 743 retired staff receiving monthly allowances, Mrs. Paist wrote, "It was a high privilege to be in at the beginning of this enterprise which has added to the dignity and well-being of the YWCA's fine professional staff."

At four successive biennial conventions of the 1920s, Mrs. Paist was elected president of the YWCA of the U.S.A., ergo, the convention's presiding officer. "In those days things were not nearly so orderly," she recalls. "Now you're elected at the end of one convention and have a year to get ready for the next. Then, one minute you were a delegate and the next you were president, and you just had to pick up raw, as it were, with nothing to hang onto but Robert's *Rules of Order!*"

Nominees were consulted rather informally beforehand about their willingness to have their names put up. When Mrs. Paist was approached on the matter in the spring of 1920, she had a seven-month-old child, Horace, the third and last of the Paist children. "I said I would *not* go to another convention with a nursing baby, but if Horace was weaned by then, I would. He was, and I went. Incidentally, he was the best-fed of our three because by that time we'd learned so much more about baby-feeding."

At the convention's opening session, the afternoon of April 13, with 2,123 voting and visiting delegates present, she was nominated by her former colleague, Harriet Taylor, and elected. "There I was, aged forty, and president of the national Association! Fortunately for me, it was the end of the session and I had until next morning to get used to the idea!"

The convention hall was "a big drafty theater—but not so big that a woman's voice couldn't carry! Excitement was kind of in the air that year, not only because of our own concerns. The woman suffrage amendment had finally passed in Congress the year before [May 21, 1919], and the state legislatures had ratified it quickly. We knew it would soon be proclaimed in effect and many of us would be voting for the first time in the fall elections. [The amendment was proclaimed in effect August 26, 1920.] We had a lot of business to transact so we didn't waste time talking about it, but it was all part of what you might call the atmosphere of the convention."

The first discussion over which Mrs. Paist presided on April 14 concerned the final vote on the change of membership basis for student Associations. She reviewed the background by which the proposal had been brought to the convention. After a full day's discussion, a ballot vote showed an eighty-five per cent affirmative vote. Students and others who spoke for the resolution made a plea for "Christian democracy" on the campuses. The somewhat vocal minority who opposed it claimed the move would be "disloyal to the great evangelical church," or associated the trend toward "brotherhood" with "subversive movements" current in the United States.

One local Association board member said the YWCA should trust its youth and their dreams because "if it were not for the dreams of yesterday's youth we would not be here today." A student representing an Association of eight hundred Negro girls ended her eloquent speech: "I came here to say 'Open up the door' ... We want Associations yet unborn to say 'Blessed are they who were present at that convention of 1920.' "

The real test of the new president's mettle came on the convention's fourth day, when a six-part proposal was introduced by Mrs. W. D. Mitchell, of St. Paul, Minnesota, chairman of the committee on the National Board's report. This proposal, remembered today chiefly for Part Two which recommended adoption of the "Social Ideals of the Churches" as the YWCA's social platform, delineated "today's challenge to Christianity" in terms of explicit social and economic reforms.

"In other words," interprets Mrs. Paist, "would we support workers to get their just dues, either through the labor movement or some other? There was a fair amount of support for a retirement plan to give security to our own staff, but for members who were working on factory jobs, it was something else again!

"Even ten or fifteen years later—our times move so fast—it would have been hard to realize what was the truth then, that even the word 'labor' was practically a dirty word and people used it sparingly. Instead they talked about social justice and how working hours and wages were a threat to workers' health and happiness. Many of our most loyal and devoted board members were caught in a terrible spot. Their husbands, especially those in business, were almost all violently opposed to yielding to any demands of working people and looked upon it as gross disloyalty that their wives should be mixed up with an organization that would take such action as we were proposing then to take. Some of them agonized over it, then bravely took a stand on what they believed was right even though, as someone has said, they were scared to go home afterward!

"Others did as one of our very rich, powerful, generous National Board members did. She got up and protested that we were losing our religion and were in danger of Communism. In 1917 I had caught on to the fact that many people were as frightened by the Russian Revolution as they were by the war. By 1920, after the Communists had come to power in Russia, fear of 'labor' and fear of Communists here at home were practically twins."

At the end of a day of heated debate, the first four of the proposal's six parts had been accepted unanimously. (The group led by the dissenting board member apparently abstained.) The next morning, the "leader of the opposition" asked for the floor and, expressing "real grief over some of the sentiments expressed and measures adopted by this Convention," resigned from membership on the National Board.

"I wasn't in the least prepared for such a thing and suddenly I felt very lonesome up there," Mrs. Paist says, remembering the tense moment.

Here is the chairman's next speech, taken from the Proceedings:

> Mrs. Paist: I do not know whether it is the function of this body to accept resignations from the National Board. I shall pass it on to the committee on laws. My personal conviction is that only the working out of what we have voiced will prove whether we have been sound or not. And I do so rejoice that we shall meet again and that these questions will all be open and we can then with more experience look into the future ...

During this speech, the resigning board member left the convention hall. A board member of a small local Association rose and said perhaps the delegates had "gone into this hotheadedly," and that the National Board member's resignation seemed a "dreadful loss."

"Before there is any more discussion," said the president briskly, "we must be talking to some resolution or motion because if you women get to just talking without one, I am going home!" After another "maybe-we-should-reconsider" speech from the floor, she again called for a motion. No one spoke. After a moment, she asked Mrs. Mitchell to continue with her report, and the last parts of the proposal were accepted unanimously.

"Mrs. Paist was a wonderful presiding officer," says a longtime member of the National Board staff. "She kept her feet on the ground, she was simple spoken, she knew when to move in and when to sit back."

For herself, Theresa Paist sums it up this way: "I put a lot into those conventions because it seemed to me a very important event when representatives of YWCAs from all over the country would come together to decide what they believed about things and what was most important to work on for the next two years. I was proud later on when somebody said to me, 'You have done something with this job that makes it worth taking.'"

$\mathcal{B}$ibliography

Burton, Margaret E. *Mabel Cratty*. New York: The Womans Press, 1929.

Chase, Mary Ellen. *Abby Aldrich Rockefeller*. New York: The Macmillan Company, 1930.

Graham, Abbie. *Grace H. Dodge*. New York: The Womans Press, 1926.

Harper, Elsie. *The Past Is Prelude* (pamphlet). National Board YWCA, 1963.

Nevins, Allan. *The Emergence of Modern America 1865-1878*. New York: The Macmillan Company, 1927.

Rice, Anna V. *A History of the World's Young Women's Christian Association*. New York: The Womans Press, 1947.

Rice, Anna V., ed. *Thoughts and Meditations*. From the Notebooks of Mary Billings French. New York, 1955.

Roberts, Richard. *Florence Simms*. New York: The Womans Press, 1926.

Schlesinger, Arthur M. *The Rise of the City 1878-1898*. New York: The Macmillan Company, 1933.

Sims, Mary S. *The First Twenty-Five Years* (Summary of work of YWCA of the U.S.A. 1906-31). New York: The Womans Press, 1932.

Sims, Mary S. *The Natural History of a Social Institution—the YWCA.* New York: J. J. Little and Ives Company, 1935.

Wheeler, W. Reginald. *A Man Sent from God: The Biography of Robert E. Speer.* Westwood, New Jersey: Fleming H. Revell Co., 1956.

Wilson, Elizabeth. *Fifty Years of Association Work Among Young Women.* New York: National Board YWCA, 1916.

Works Progress Administration, Federal Writers Project. *Vermont—A Guide to the Green Mountain State.* Boston: Houghton Mifflin Co., 1937.

Young Women's Christian Association, National Board:

In Memory of Grace H. Dodge, reprint from *The Association Monthly,* Vol. IX, No. 2, Section II

Historical Files

Proceedings, Conventions of 1920, 1960, 1964

Report of War Work Council, 1920

The YWCA Magazine, Centennial Issue, Jan. 1953